REEDS DICTIONARY

OF

SHIPPING AND
MARINE FINANCE

REEDS DICTIONARY

OF

SHIPPING AND MARINE FINANCE

HONORÉ C PAELINCK

ADLARD COLES NAUTICAL
London

Published by Adlard Coles Nautical
an imprint of A & C Black Publishers Ltd
36 Soho Square, London W1D 3QY
www.adlardcoles.com

First edition published 2010

First published by Pandora Publishers NV under the title
Glossary of Shipping and Financial Terms

Copyright © Pandora Publishers and Honoré C Paelinck 2008

ISBN 978-1-4081-2442-0

A CIP catalogue record for this book is available from the British
Library.

This book is produced using paper that is made from wood
grown in managed, sustainable forests. It is natural, renewable
and recyclable. The logging and manufacturing processes conform
to the environmental regulations of the country of origin.

Typeset in 9/11pt RotisSansSerif Light by
Palimpsest Book Production Limited, Grangemouth, Stirlingshire
Printed and bound in Spain by GraphyCems

Note: while all reasonable care has been taken in the publication
of this book, the publisher takes no responsibility for the use of
the methods or products described in the book.

CONTENTS

FOREWORD

'Everything has to be presented in the simplest possible way, but not simpler than that'
Albert Einstein

In marine finance and insurance, money markets, securities and banking, new words, methods and systems are constantly being developed, and acronyms, abbreviations and sometimes bizarre or comical names are frequently used in contracts and agreements. It is therefore increasingly important to understand the growing body of terminology and jargon.

Students wanting to learn more about maritime and port economics have not always been prepared to gain a detailed knowledge of the specific vocabulary of the shipping world. This glossary of unfamiliar terms will enable everyone to gain a quicker and better understanding of these new terms.

This dictionary is a comprehensive reference to shipping and financial terminology, and is organized so that the information is clear, understandable and readily accessible. It certainly does not pretend to be exhaustive but should inspire readers to look further in a world where continuous learning is a must.

There is nothing constant in the universe
All ebb and flow and every shape that's born
Bears in its womb the seeds of change.
Ovid

SHIPPING TERMS

A for ALFA   Morse = (. –)
As a flag it means 'Undergoing speed trials.'
Burgee flag = white at hoist, blue at the fly.

AA Always afloat (chartering).

AAOSA Always afloat or safe aground. The condition for a vessel whilst in port.

AAR Against all risk.

ABAFT Towards the stern of the vessel.

ABANDONMENT Leaving the ship as unseaworthy; giving up possession of a vessel and cargo to establish a claim on the underwriters.

ABEAM In line at right angles to the vessel's length, opposite the centre of the vessel's side.

ABI Association of British Insurers.

ABLE BODIED SEAMAN A member of the deck crew who is able to perform all the duties of an experienced seaman; certificated by examination; must have three years' sea service. Also called Able Seaman and AB.

ABS American Bureau of Shipping. A US-based private classification or standards setting society for merchant ships and other marine systems.

ACCOMMODATION UNIT Fitted with cabins and catering facilities for offshore crews. Semi-submersible accommodation units are often called 'Flotels'.

ACETYLENE A colourless gas, highly inflammable, liberated by the chemical action of water on calcium carbide.

ACT OF GOD Accidents arising from physical causes (lightning, earthquakes, hurricanes, plagues etc) and not from human agency.

ADDENDUM Additional terms at the end of a charter party.

ADMEASUREMENT The confirmed or official dimensions of a ship.

ADN Accord du transport Dangereux par voie Navigable.

ADNR ADN pour le Rhin (River Rhine).

ADR AD par Route (road).

ADRIFT Floating at random.

AD VALOREM DUTY A percentage of the market value of the goods in the country from which they are imported.

ADVANCE NOTES Draft on owner or agent of a vessel for wages, given to seamen.

ADVENTURE Goods consigned to a party to be disposed of to best advantage. Speculation in which consignor takes all risk.

ADVICE Formal notice of commercial transactions.

AF Advanced Freights.

AFAA As Far As Applicable.

AFFREIGHTMENT A contract for the carriage of goods by sea for payment, expressed in a charter party or bill of lading.

AFFRETEUR (French) Charterer.

AFRAMAX Crude and product tankers with a deadweight between 45,000 and 100,000 tons.

AFT In, near or toward the stern of the vessel.

AFTERPEAK Enclosed part in the rear part of the vessel for storekeeping or as a tank for drinking water or ballast.

AGENCY FEE A fee charged to the ship by the ship's agent, representing payment for services while the ship was in port. Sometimes called attendance fee.

AGENT One who represents a principal or buys or sells for another. No agent in the course of his agency and in the matter of his agency can be allowed to make any profit without the knowledge and consent of his principal; this is an inflexible rule.

AGROUND Applied to a vessel touching the bottom.

AHT Anchor Handling Tug. Moves anchors and tows drilling vessels, lighters and similar.

AHTS Anchor Handling Tug/Supply. Combined supply and anchor-handling ship.

AID Agency for International Development in the USA.

AIMS American Institute of Merchant Shipping.

AIRDRAFT The vertical distance between the water level and the highest part of the ship above, the top of the highest mast.

ALDIS LAMP Lamp with focused beam for

signalling with Morse code, can be seen at a distance of up to 20 miles. Still used for attracting attention at night.

ALFALFA A herbaceous plant belonging to the clover family. Cultivated in Argentina for fodder for cattle, sheep or horses. A bale of alfalfa weighs 50kg.

ALKANET A plant of which the root yields a red dye used in colouring oils, wood dyeing etc.

ALLIANCE Conglomerate of different shipping companies who agree on shipping lanes, frequencies of sailing and general tariff terms and conditions. The alliance is not restricted to one geographical region but can cover the whole world.

ALLISION The act of striking or collision by a moving vessel against a stationary object.

ALOES The expressed juice of the leaves and stem of a plant which yields a fibre known as sisal hemp of vegetable silk. The juice has an aromatic smell and a bitter taste.

ALOFT Above, overhead.

ALRS Admiralty List of Radio Signals: British Admiralty publications (8 volumes, some in double or triple books) informing navigators about all the radio stations and various kinds of broadcast information such as time signals, weather and navigational warnings, positioning systems and VTS procedures. Updated through Weekly Notices to Mariners.

AMBERGRIS An unpleasant looking odoriferous substance ejected by the cachalot whale. Valued as a perfume and as an aromatic stimulant.

AMC American Maritime Congress.

AMIDSHIPS Generally in the middle portion of a vessel.

AMMONIA (ANHYDROUS) NH_3 Gas usually carried by LPG tankers at about -50 degrees Celsius. Lighter than air, it escapes easily from any opening and is highly dangerous to inhale in great quantity. Reacts violently with water. Boiling point -33, melting point -78, auto-ignition 630, all in degrees Celsius. Molecular weight 17, flammable range 15 – 26 –1 pc.

AMVER Automated Mutual Assistance Vessel Rescue System.

ANF Arrival Notification Form. A document that advises the consignee or container operator that goods or containers have arrived at port of discharge (BIMCO).

AOE Any One Event.

AOR Any One Risk.

AP Additional Premium.

API American Petroleum Institute.

APOLLINARIS An alkaline mineral water containing carbonates of soda, derived from the Apollinaris spring in the valley of the Ahr, in the Rhine province.

APPROACHES The access to the port via a dredged channel marked by buoys and beacons.

APT Aft Peak Tank.

A/R All Risks.

ARBITRATION Method of settling disputes without going to court, usually binding on parties. A clause usually in a charter party.

ARCS Admiralty Raster Chart Service. Electronic display of nautical charts.

ARPA Automated Radar Plotting Aid. System to assist the watch-keeper using the radar for collision prevention.

ARREST The detention of a vessel with a view to her ultimate release when the purpose of the arrest has been fulfilled.

ARTICLES OF AGREEMENT The document containing all particulars relating to the terms of agreement between the Master of the vessel and the crew. Sometimes called ship's articles, shipping articles.

A/S After sight, alongside, account sales.

ASBA American Shipbrokers Association.

ASSESSOR A person who officially estimates the value of goods for the purpose of apportioning the sum payable by the underwriters to settle claims made for non-marine and fire losses. *See average adjuster.*

ASSIGNEE Party to whom any right or property is assigned.

ASSIGNMENT An absolute transfer of property.

ASSIGNOR Party who assigns or makes over his interest in property to another.

ASSUMPSIT An action at law wherein the plaintiff asserts that the defendant undertook to carry out a certain act but failed to fulfil his promise. In the USA, the most common form of action. Now superseded by 'action for breach of contract'.

ASSURED The party indemnified against loss by means of insurance.

ASTERN A backward direction in the line of a vessel's fore and aft line; behind. If a vessel moves backwards it is said to move astern; opposite to ahead.

ASTM American Society for Testing and Materials. The world's largest source of voluntary consensus standards for materials, products, systems and services. Used mainly on tankers.

ATDNSHINC Any Time Day or Night Sundays & Holidays Included.

ATHWARTSHIPS Across the width of the vessel. At a right angle with the fore and aft line.

AT SEA In marine insurance this phrase applies to a ship which is free from its moorings and ready to sail.

ATTERBERG LIMITS Limits of liquidity, plasticity and solidity.

ATTESTATION The legal act of witnessing a deed by affixing one's signature thereto.

AUTOMATIC PILOT An instrument designed to control automatically a vessel's steering gear so that she follows a pre-determined track through the water.

AVERAGE When the sum insured is less than the value of the property, the assured becomes his own insurer for the excess value and has therefore to bear his share of any loss that may occur rateably with the underwriter or company. Average in all cases means loss.

AVERAGE ADJUSTER A qualified person engaged in making statements to the liability of underwriters and others concerned in connection with marine losses or damages, and to draw up the apportionment of General Average between ship, freight and cargo.

AVERAGE BOND A formal acknowledgment of liability to pay the proportion of general average losses or expenses due from any particular interest when such proportion has been properly determined by adjustment.

AVERAGE STATEMENT Average adjuster's statement.

AVOIRDUPOIS System of weights in which 1lb equals 16oz.

AWIWL Always Within Institute Warranties Limits. For insurance purpose the ship should sail only within sea areas in which she is always insured. The Bering Sea is outside these limits although the southern part of it is almost always free of ice. Underwriters are often asking an extra premium to enter it.

AWO American Waterway Operators. The national trade association for the barge and towing industry and the shipyards employed in the repair and construction of these craft.

B

B for BRAVO   **Morse = (– . . .)**
Flag = red.
As a flag it means 'I am discharging/loading explosives or inflammable substances'. Widely used when bunkering.

BACKFREIGHT The owners of a ship are entitled to payment as freight for merchandise returned through the fault of either the consignees or the consignors. Such payment, which is over and above the normal freight, is called backfreight.

BACKHAUL A deviation to move cargo on the return leg of a voyage for the purpose of minimizing ballast mileage and thereby reducing transportation costs. Also: to haul a shipment back over a part of a route that it has already travelled; return movement of cargo.

BACKHOE, EXCAVATOR Handling device for removing sand or debris and to load trucks or barges. Also used for very accurate dredging alongside quay walls.

BACKLETTER Where a seller/shipper issues a 'letter of indemnity' in favour of the carrier in exchange for a clean bill of lading. May have only a limited value. Example: P & I problems.

BAF Bunker adjustment factor.

BAGGED CARGO Various kinds of commodities usually packed in sacks or in bags, such as sugar, cement, milk powder, onions, grain, flour etc.

BAILMENT Delivery of goods in trust.

BALE CAPACITY Cubic capacity of a vessel's holds to carry packaged dry cargo such as bales/pallets.

BALLAST Heavy substances loaded by a vessel to improve stability, trimming, sea-keeping and to increase the immersion at the propeller. Sea water ballast is commonly pumped in most vessels in ballast tanks, positioned in compartments right at the bottom and in some cases on the sides, called wing tanks. On a tanker, ballast is sea water that is taken into the cargo tanks to submerge the vessel to a proper trim and give 'bite' to the propeller.

BALLAST BONUS Compensation above the chartering price for relatively long ballast voyage to reach loading port.

BALLAST KEEL Heavy keel fitted to sailing vessels to lower the centre of gravity and improve stability.

BALLAST MOVEMENT A voyage or voyage leg made without any paying cargo in a vessel's tanks. To maintain proper stability, trim, or draft, sea water is usually carried during such movements.

BALLAST TANKS Compartments at the bottom of a ship or on the sides which are filled with liquids for stability and to make the ship seaworthy. Any shipboard tank or compartment on a tanker normally used for carrying (salt) water ballast. When these compartments or tanks are not connected with the cargo system they are called segregated ballast tanks or systems.

BAR DRAUGHT Vessel's maximum draught to cross a bar.

BARE BOAT CHARTER A charter in which the bare ship is chartered without crew; the charterer, for a stipulated sum, takes over the vessel for a stated period of time with a minimum of restrictions; the charterer appoints the Master and the crew and pays all running expenses.

BARGE Flat-bottomed boat designed to carry cargo on inland waterways, with or without engines or crew accommodation. The capacity varies between 100 and 6,000 tons. Barges without engines can also be lashed together in convoy and either pushed or pulled by tugs, carrying cargo from 18,000 tons on the Rhine in Europe to 60,000 tons or more on the Mississippi-Missouri. Small barges for carrying cargo between ship and shore are known as lighters.

BARGE CARRIERS Ships designed to carry either barges or containers exclusively, or some variable number of barges and containers simultaneously. Currently this class includes two types of vessels, the LASH and the SeaBee.

BARRATRY A fraudulent act on the part of the Master or crew against the vessel and cargo without the agreement of the ship owner.

BARREL 42 US gallons (3.785 litres) at 60° Fahrenheit (15.5° Celsius) = 159 litres. Also 35 Imperial gallons.

BASIC SLAG A by-product of the manufacture of steel. Used as a fertilizer.

BATTEN Board 6 feet long or more, at least 2 inches thick and 4 to 8 inches broad, used for flooring; strip of wood used for securing hatchway tarpaulin, so preventing sea water entering the hold.

BAUXITE Raw material required for the production of aluminium. It is an impure hydrated oxide of aluminium. Used for the manufacture of fire-bricks and crucibles and for lining furnaces requiring intense heat. When thoroughly dehydrated it acts as a decolourizing agent for mineral oils and waxes. Yields alum and other aluminium salts.

BB Below Bridges. Bulbous Bow.

BBB Before Breaking Bulk. Refers to freight payments that must be received before discharge of a vessel commences.

BBLS Barrels.

BC CODE Code of safe practice for solid bulk cargoes (IMO).

BCH CODE Bulk Chemical Code. Construction rules for chemical tankers built between 12 April 1972 and 30 June 1982, after which IBC Code has to be considered.

BD Bar Draught.

B/D Barrels per Day (measure of petroleum production).

BDI Both Days Inclusive.

BDL Barge Discharge List.

BDLS Bundles.

BDS Broker's Daily Statement.

BDS Boards.

BE Bill of Exchange. Bill of Entry.

BEACON Navigation aid along river, fixed on bed or bank. Going upstream red beacons on the left side, green on the right side. Red beacons have flat tops, green have pointed tops.

BEAM The width of a ship. Also called breadth.

BELT LINE A switching railway operating within the port or commercial area.

BENEFICIAL OWNERSHIP Designates the owner who receives the benefits or profits from the operation.

BENZENE A distillate from coal tar.

BENZINE A distillate from petroleum.

BENZOL Term synonymous with benzene.

BERTH A place in which a vessel is moored or secured; place alongside a quay where a ship loads or discharges cargo.

BERTHAGE Charges for the use of a berth.

BERTH CARGO When a liner cargo vessel accepts extra cargo to fill up the empty space remaining.

BERTH C/P Term used in a voyage charter party, eg 'vessel shall proceed to Berth 2 at Falmouth.'

BERTH TERM Shipped under a rate that does not include the cost of loading or unloading.

BESMA Belgian Shipmasters' Association. Professional association of shipmasters legally recognized by decision of the Belgian Council of State of 29 November 1977. Main international objective: safety of shipping and promotion of the profession.

BH Bordeaux to Hamburg inclusive. Bill of Health.

BIA British Insurance Association.

BIBA British Insurance Brokers Association.

BIFFEX Baltic International Freight Futures Exchange.

BILGE The breadth of a ship's bottom or the part of the floor which approaches to a horizontal direction on which she would rest if aground. When this part of a ship is fractured she is said to be 'bilged'.

BILLETS Rough steel bars with smaller square section but longer than blooms.

BILL OF LADING, B/L. A negotiable document by which the Master of a ship acknowledges having received in good order and condition (or the reverse) certain specified goods consigned to him by some particular shipper and binds himself to deliver them in similar condition, unless the perils of the sea, fire or enemies prevent him, to the consignees of the shippers at the point of destination on their paying him the stipulated freight. A bill of lading specifies the name of the ship, the Master, the port of loading and destination of the ship, the goods, the consignee, and the rate of freight.

BILL OF SALE, B/S A registered transfer of goods to a person for some consideration, empowering him to dispose of them upon non-fulfilment of certain conditions. A bill of sale is void and of no effect unless registered in accordance with statute.

BIMCO Baltic and International Maritime Council. Founded in 1905, located in Copenhagen (Denmark), has 2650 members in 110 countries: ship owners, brokers, agents, P&I clubs.

BLACK CARGO Cargo banned by general cargo workers for some reason. This ban could be because the cargo is dangerous or hazardous to health.

BLACK GANG A slang expression referring to the personnel in the engine department aboard ship.

BLACK SHOE US Navy expression for a Naval Officer originating from the navy (as opposed to 'brown shoe' who can become a Naval Officer but originates in the air force as a pilot).

BLEVE Boiling Liquid Expanding Vapour Explosion.

BLK Bulk.

BLOOMS Rough rolled square bars of half worked steel with sides 5 inches and larger. Supplied in shorter lengths than billets.

BLS Bureau of Labour Statistics. Department of Labour.

BLT Built. Year in which the ship was built. At times ships older than 15 years cannot be accepted for chartering.

BLUE PETER Flag P of International Signal Code. Signal to call crew and passengers back to the ship before sailing.

B/N Booking Note.

BOARDS Softwood from 1.5 to 2 inches thick and 6 to 9 inches broad.

BOATSWAIN (BOSUN) The highest unlicensed rating in the deck department who has immediate charge of all deck hands and who in turn comes under the direct orders of the Master, Chief Mate or Mate.

BOD Biochemical Oxygen Demand. The amount of oxygen required during the decomposition of organic matter by aerobic microbiological action. Water body polluted by biologically degradable organic matter loses some or all of its dissolved oxygen by the respiratory oxygen demand of the micro-organisms consuming the organic matter. BOD 5 (5 days of BOD at 20°C) is a common measure of biodegradable pollution in water.

BOGIE Set of wheels under a railway wagon, locomotive or truck.

BOILERS Steam generating units used aboard ship to provide steam for propulsion (and) for heating and other auxiliary purposes.

BOLTER An instrument or machine for bolting of sifting flour, meal etc as a piece of bolting cloth, a sieve or a bolting machine.

BONDED WAREHOUSE Warehouse authorized by customs authorities for storage of goods on which payment of duties is deferred until the goods are removed.

BOND PORT Port of a vessel's initial customs entry to any country; also known as first port of call.

BOO Build-Own-Operate. Form of project wherein a private party or consortium agrees to finance, construct, operate and maintain a facility previously owned and/or operated by a public authority. The concessionaire retains ownership of the facility. He also bears the commercial risk of operating the facility.

BOOKING NOTE Document prepared by the ship's agent containing a list of the already accepted cargo to be loaded on board.

BORA A strong NE wind in the Adriatic.

BORE A tidal flood which rushes up the mouth of a river and, meeting the ebb tide or opposing current, forms a wall of water which increases in height as the river narrows.

BOT Build-Operate-Transfer. A form of concession wherein a private party or consortium agrees to finance, construct, operate and maintain a facility for a specified period and then transfer the facility to a government or other public authority. The concessionaire bears the commercial risk of operating the facility.

BOTTOMRY Money borrowed on a vessel's hull, freight and cargo, to be repaid with interest only if the vessel returns safely. The lender of the money has an insurance interest in respect of the loan. Any instrument of bottomry not occasioned and justified by inevitable necessity is void.

BOW Front part of the ship that cuts through the water.

BOW THRUSTER A propeller at the underwater part of the bow of the ship which turns at right angles to the fore-and-aft line and thus provides transverse thrust as a manœuvring aid, as opposed to 'stern thrusters'.

B/P or BOP Balance of Payments.

B/R Bills Receivable.

BRAN The husk of wheat, barely, oats or other grain separated from the flour after milling. The coarsest portion of the ground husk.

BREADTH *See Beam.*

BREAK BULK Loose non-containerized cargo stowed directly into a ship's hold. The process of assimilating many small shipments into one large shipment at a central point so that economies of scale may be achieved. As a verb means to commence discharge of cargo.

BREAKBULK VESSEL A general, multipurpose, cargo ship that carriers cargoes of non uniform sizes, often on pallets, resulting in labour-intensive loading and unloading; calls at various ports to pick up different kinds of cargoes.

BREAK STRENGTH Load on a chain, wire or rope at which it will break, varies between 6 and 12 times the Safe Working Load (SWL).

BREAKWATER Protective construction at a port or its approaches against breaking waves or storm winds. Constructed with rock and concrete blocks and solidly anchored in the sea floor.

BRIDGE Used to refer to the navigating section of the vessel where the wheelhouse and chart room are located; erected structure at the front, amidships or aft of the main deck of a ship to accommodate the wheelhouse.

BRIQUETTES Fuel made of fine coal dust (duff) with 7 to 9% of gas pitch added to bind it together.

BRITISH THERMAL UNIT (BT(h)U) Unit of heat. Amount of heat required to raise one pound of pure water one degree F or from 39.1° to 40.1°F.

BROACH TO A ship is said to be broached to when she veers or swerves suddenly so as to bring her broadside to wind and sea.

BROKER A person who transacts the business of negotiating between merchants and ship owners respecting cargoes and clearances; he also effects insurances with the underwriters.

BROKERAGE FEE Percentage of freight payable to broker (by owners in c/ps) or applicable to sale or purchase.

BRONZE A mixture of copper, zinc, tin and lead used for castings etc.

BROWN GOODS Cargo consisting of radios and TVs.

BROWN SHOE Pilot who converts to the navy to become a Naval Officer. *See also Black shoe.*

BS Boiler Survey.

B/S Bill of Sale.

BS/L Bills of Lading.

BST British Summer Time.

B TO B Both to Blame (collision clause).

BULB, BULBOUS BOW Protrusion under the waterline at the front of the ship's hull, built to influence the direction in which the water molecules rotate in the forward movement, helping the ship to a higher speed.

BULK Cargo shipped in loose condition and of a homogeneous nature. Cargoes that are shipped unpacked either dry, such as grain and ore, or liquid, such as petroleum products, vegetable oils or chemicals. Bulk service generally is not provided on a regularly scheduled basis but rather as needed, on specialized ships, transporting a specific commodity. Chemical tankers may transport a number of different products.

BULK CARRIER Ship specifically designed to transport vast amounts of dry or liquid cargoes such as sugar, grain, wine, ore, chemicals, liquefied natural gas, coal and oil. *See also LNG carrier, Tanker, OBO ship.*

BULKHEAD A name given to any vertical partition which separates different compartments of the ship or spaces from one another.

BUNKER The space in which fuel for the propulsion of the vessel is stored. To bunker: to replenish the fuel.

BUNKERS Fuel consumed by the engines of a ship; stored in compartments or tanks in a ship for fuel storage.

BUOY A floating object employed as an aid to mariners to mark the navigable limits of channels, their fairways, sunken dangers, isolated rocks, telegraph cables and the like; floating devices fixed in place in sea, lake or river as reference points for navigation or for other purposes. Going upstream, red beacons are on the left side and are flat topped, green on the right side with pointed tops.

BUTANE C_4H_{10} Petroleum gas carried on LPG tankers. Flash point = -60, boiling point = -0.5, auto-ignition = 410, all in degrees Celsius. Molecular weight = 58. Flammable range = 1 – 9pc.

BV Bureau Veritas. Classification Society in France (Paris).

BWT Bleeding Wing Tanks. In order to load the ship to full capacity with grain, the top ballast tanks are sometimes used as cargo spaces. Bleeding holes, normally closed by flanges when the tank is ballasted, allow the cargo to fall in the hold underneath, filling all the space available. This method of loading, however, involves a lot of extra preparation work and a lot of cleaning after the discharge.

C

●●●●●●●●●●●●●●●●●●●●●●●●●●●●

C for CHARLIE   Morse = (– . – .)
Flag = horizontally divided into 5 stripes. Blue above
and under, red in the middle between two white
ones. When hoisted singly from a ship it means 'Yes
– Affirmative'.

●●●●●●●●●●●●●●●●●●●●●●●●●●●●

C_3H_8 *See Propane*
C_4H_{10} *See Butane*
CABLE SHIP, CABLE LAYER A specially
constructed ship for the laying and repairing of
telegraph and telephone cables across channels,
seas, lakes and oceans.

CABOTAGE The carriage of goods or passengers
for remuneration, taken on at one point and
discharged at another point within the territory of
the same country. Frequently reserved for national
flag vessels of that nation.

CABOTAGE POLICIES Reservation of a country's
coastal (domestic) shipping for its own flag vessels.

CACAO The dried seeds or beans of the cocoa tree
Theobroma cacao grown in West Africa, the West
Indies and Central and South American states.

CAF Currency Adjustment Factor.

CALCIUM CARBIDE A crystalline solid, colourless
when pure but often resembling limestone.
Produced by heating lime and carbon together in an
electric furnace. Used for generating acetylene, a
powerful illuminating gas. A drum of calcium
carbide should never be opened by hammer and
chisel as an explosion may result, and no naked light
should be allowed near the generator or the storage
carbide container.

CALX Chalk or lime. The friable substance left when
a metal has been subjected to calcinations or
combustion by heat. Metallic calxes are called oxides.

CAMPHOR A whitish translucent crystalline
volatile drug with aromatic smell and bitter taste.
Obtained from trees indigenous to Japan and the
Eastern Archipelago.

C&F Cost and Freight. Seller pays cost and freight
but no insurance. The buyer or consignee pays the
expenses for unloading, lighterage, wharfage,
cartage, duties etc.

C&I Cost and Insurance.

CANT To turn or take an inclined position.

CAORF Computer-Assisted Operations Research Facility. A Maritime Administration R&D facility located at the US Merchant Marine Academy, Kings Point, New York.

CAP Condition Assessment Programme. Structural assessment programme devised by the classification societies ABS, LR and DNV.

CAPSTAN A vertical revolving drum, spool-shaped, power driven or operated by manpower. Used for hauling in or letting out of hawsers and anchors.

CARFLOAT Barge equipped with tracks on which railway wagons are moved by water.

CARGO BATTENS Wooden planking in the holds to protect cargo from contact with the vessel's steel plating and frames.

CARGO HANDLING The act of loading and discharging a cargo ship, also called stevedoring.

CARGO PLAN A plan giving the location, quantities and description of the various products carried in the ship's cargo holds, after the loading is completed.

CARGO PREFERENCE Reserving a portion of a nation's imports and exports to national flag vessels.

CARGO RETENTION CLAUSES Clauses introduced by charterers based on shortage of delivered cargo because of increased oil prices.

CARGO TONNAGE Ocean freight is frequently billed on the basis of weight or measurement tons. Weight tons can be expressed in terms of short tons of 2000lbs, long tons in tons of 2240lbs or metric tons of 1000 kilograms (2204.62 pounds). Measurement tons are usually expressed as cargo measurement of 40 cubic feet (1.12 cubic metres) or cubic metres (35.3 cubic feet). The expression for billing is 'weight or measurement whichever is the greater', then called 'freight ton'.

CARRIAGE OF GOODS BY SEA ACT A law enacted in 1936 covering the transportation of merchandise by sea to or from ports of the United States and in foreign trades.

CARRIER Any person or entity who, in a contract of carriage, undertakes to perform or to procure the performance of carriage by sea, inland waterway, rail, road, air or a combination of such modes. Owner or operator of vessels providing transportation to shippers. The term is also used to refer to the vessels.

CARTAGE Intra-port or local hauling of cargo by drays or trucks; also referred to as drayage.

CASSAVA The tuber from the manioc plant from which tapioca is obtained.

CASSIA BARK Bark of a number of trees of the cinnamon species in Sri Lanka and other islands of the East.

CATAMARAN A double hulled vessel constructed in steel, wood, aluminium or reinforced glassfibre and is also composed of two hulls diagonally joined together by various methods. Normally no ballast is needed to counteract the centre buoyancy since it enjoys good stability at sea. Mainly used for higher speed.

CATUG Short for Catamaran Tug. A rigid catamaran tug connected to a barge. When joined together they form and look like a single hull of a ship; ocean going integrated tug-barge vessels.

CATWALK A raised bridge construction running fore and aft, also called 'walkway'. It affords safe passage over the pipelines and other deck obstructions.

CAUSA PROXIMA (Latin) The immediate or final cause of accident or damage. The question which is the 'causa proxima' of a loss can only arise where there is a succession of causes.

CAUSTIC SODA Consists chiefly of sodium carbonate. Shipped in iron drums. The holds must be quite dry as it is very corrosive when in contact in a wet condition with ironwork. Used in rubber, tanning, soap, textile and paper industries and in refining petroleum and vegetable oils.

CAVEAT EMPTOR (Latin) Let the buyer beware. The seller, in effect, says 'There are the goods, examine them for yourself'. The seller does not take responsibility for the condition of the title of the goods sold.

CBF Cubic Feet.

CBM Cubic Metres.

CBT (MARPOL) Clean Ballast Tank. Tank exclusively dedicated to clean ballast.

CC Civil Commotions. Cancellation Clause.

CCC Commodity Credit Corporation.

CCE Credit Controlling Entity. Bank, insurance or any other.

CCF Capital Construction Fund. A tax benefit for operators of US-built, US-flag ships in the US foreign, Great Lakes or non-contiguous domestic trades, by which taxes may be deferred on income deposited in a fund to be used for the replacement of vessels.

CCTV Closed Circuit Television. Method of inspecting the underwater part of the ship while recording a video at the same time.

CD Chart Datum. Plane of reference to which all depths and heights are referred. Usually it is the MLW, except in France and Spain where it is the Lowest Low Water possible.

CDI Chemical Distribution Institute. Inspection scheme of tankers following the rules of the Council of Europe Federation of Chemical Industries.

CDS Construction Differential Subsidy. A direct subsidy paid to US shipyards building US-flag ships to offset high construction costs in American shipyards. An amount of subsidy (up to 50%) is determined by estimates of construction cost differentials between US and foreign yards.

CELLULOSE Substance forming solid framework of plants. The pulp of wood used in paper making.

CENSA Council of European and Japanese National Ship owners Association.

CERTIFICATE OF INSURANCE Document generally issued where goods that are the subject of a CIF sale are insured by floating policy covering other goods as well as the particular goods in question.

CESSER CLAUSE Clause by which the charterer is relieved from liabilities accruing after the shipment of the cargo.

CERTIFICATE OF REGISTRY A document specifying the national registry of the vessel.

CEU Car Equivalent Unit. To assess the carrying capacity of car carriers.

CFC Chlorofluorocarbons. A family of inert, non-toxic and easily liquefied chemicals used in refrigeration, air conditioning, packaging, insulation or as solvents and aerosol propellants. Because CFCs are not destroyed in the lower atmosphere they drift into the upper atmosphere where their chlorine components destroy ozone. The gas used in most ship refrigerating plants, including containers, was the freon R22, also a CFC, and thus had to be replaced.

CFO Coast or Channel For Orders.

CFR Code of Federal Rules (US). US laws, many of them of the utmost importance for the ship Master. Quite often all the volumes related to shipping can be found on board. The CFR is divided into titles. The following titles may be useful when following this guideline: Title 40 – Contains

Environmental Protection Agency regulations. Title 49 – Contains Department of Transportation (DOT) regulations. Changes to the regulations are published in the Federal Register. These publications can be ordered through the US Government Printing Office.

CG, CGC Container Gantry (Crane).

CGA Cargo's proportion of GA.

CH$_4$ *See Methane*

CHABE Charterers Agents Both Ends.

CHANDLER A person who deals in the selling of provisions on board ships.

CHARTERER A person to whom is given the use of the whole of the carrying capacity of a ship for the transportation of cargo or passengers to a stated port for a specified time.

CHARTERING BROKERS Those who find charters for ships or ships for employment.

CHARTER PARTY, CP Agreement by the ship owner to carry goods or to furnish a ship for that purpose, usually arranged by a broker, whereby a ship is chartered (hired) either for one voyage or a period of time.

CHARTER RATES The tariff applied for chartering tonnage in a particular trade.

CHASSIS Frame of wheels and container locking devices to secure the container for movement.

CHEMICAL TANKER Specially designed for the transport of chemicals.

CHIEF ENGINEER The Senior Engineer Officer responsible for the satisfactory working and upkeep of the main and auxiliary machinery and boiler plant on board ship.

CHIEF MATE The officer in the deck department next in rank to the Master, second in command of a ship. He is next to the Master, especially in the navigation and as far as the deck department is concerned. The Chief Mate assumes the position of the Master in his absence.

CHILLIES Small pungent pods or fruit of the capsicum genus. Grown in east Africa. Used to make cayenne pepper.

CHIPS Name for the carpenter on board ship.

CHOPT Charterers option.

CHROME ORE Mineral used for smelting and calico printing. In combination with steel forms chrome-steel with specific hardness.

CIF Cost, Insurance and Freight: Export term in which the price quoted by the exporter includes the costs of ocean transportation to the port of destination and insurance coverage.

CIF&E Cost, Insurance, Freight and Exchange.

CIFCI Cost, Insurance, Freight, Commission and Interest.

CIF CONTRACT Contract for the sale of goods which have to be carried overseas. The price quoted includes cost, insurance and freight and the sale is performed by the delivery of the relevant documents (bill of lading, invoice and insurance cover).

CIF LANDED For heavy cargo it is advisable to add the word 'landed' as extra costs may arise if the ship is not equipped to put cargo ashore and heavy lift cranes are not available.

CIFLT Cost, Insurance and Freight London Terms.

CINNAMON The inner bark of the cinnamon tree of Sri Lanka.

CLASSIFICATION SOCIETY Worldwide experienced and reputable societies which undertake to arrange inspections and advize on the hull and machinery of a ship. A private organization that supervizes vessels during their construction and afterwards in respect of their seaworthiness and the placing of vessels in grades or 'classes' according to the society's rules for each particular type. It is not compulsory by law that a ship owner have his vessel built according to the rules of any classification society but, in practice, the difficulty in securing satisfactory insurance rates for an un-classed vessel makes it a commercial obligation.

CLASSIFICATION YARD Railway yard with many tracks used for assembling freight trains.

CLEANING IN TRANSIT Stopping or articles (such as farm products) for cleaning at a point between the point of origin and destination.

CLEAN SHIP Refers to tankers that have their cargo tanks free of traces of the dark persistent oils that remain after carrying crude and heavy fuel oils.

CLEARANCE Custom House Officer's permission for a vessel to leave port, denoting that all formalities have been observed and all dues paid.

CLEAR DAYS Time to be reckoned exclusive of the first and the last days.

CLEAT Device secured on the floor of a container to provide additional support or strength to cargo-restraining device, or device attached to a wharf to secure mooring lines.

CLECAT European Association for Forwarding, Transport, Logistics and Customs Services. It represents the vast majority of national organizations of freight forwarders and customs agents both in the European Union and on a continental level.

CLOVES Pungent aromatic dried buds of the clove tree. Strongly fragrant and yielding an oil.

COA Contract Of Affreightment.

COASTER Vessel used for seagoing transport along the coast. It can use a limited prescribed distance outside the coastline. Existing for dry cargo and for liquids. Capacity goes up to 5,000t DW. Some modern coasters have a low height profile so that they can go under bridges and reach destinations far inland.

COASTWISE Domestic shipping routes along a single coast.

COBALT Grey metal similar in many respect to nickel; deep blue pigment is made from it but also used in many combinations.

COCOA *See Cacao.*

CODE OF LINER CONDUCT (UNCTAD) A convention drafted under the auspices of the United Nations Conference on Trade and Development which provides that all shipping traffic between two foreign countries is to be regulated as far as the quantities of shipments are concerned on the following percentages: 40% for owners of the country of origin, 40% for owners of country of destination and 20% for owners of the country which is neither the origin nor the destination.

COF Certificate Of Financial Responsibility (USA). Documents checked and approved by the USCG certifying that any vessel calling in the USA has a valid P&I coverage in case of pollution.

COFFERDAM A watertight structure fixed to a vessel's side to allow repairs below the waterline. A watertight enclosure for obtaining a dry foundation for piers etc.

COGSA Carriage Of Goods by Sea.

COLLATERAL SECURITY Security given above main security, supplementary security.

COLLIER Vessel used for transporting coal.

COLLISION AVOIDANCE SYSTEM Electronic system commonly used to prevent collisions in inland navigable waterways. The system is being extended to some seagoing vessels.

COLLISION BULKHEAD The foremost reinforced bulkhead just aft of the forepeak. A strong bulkhead usually located 5% of the ship's length astern of the stem. It is only pierced by piping which is usually closed by valves. Designed to prevent a ship from flooding after a head-on collision. Unfortunately, side damage due to collision also occurs and they can bring about a dramatic quick foundering of the vessel (such as when the *Mineral Dampier* was rammed by the *Hanjin Madras*).

COLLOIDAL FUEL A combination product of coal dust and oil.

COLREG Convention On International Regulations for Preventing Collisions at Sea.

COMBI Combination passenger/cargo vessel; a vessel specifically designed to carry both containers and conventional cargoes.

COMBO SHIPS Ships that can carry both liquid and dry bulk cargoes.

COMMISSION *See Brokerage fee.*

COMMON CARRIER A transportation company that provides service to the general public at published rates. Holds itself out for hire to the general public. Must post rates and cannot discriminate against customers whose cargo it is equipped to carry.

COMPLEMENT The number of Officers and crew employed upon a vessel for its safe navigation and operation.

CONBULK, CONTAINER/BULK CARRIER Vessel able to carry either containers or dry bulk cargoes.

CONCESSION Arrangement whereby a private party (concessionaire) leases assets from a public authority for an extended period and has responsibility for financing specified new fixed investments during the period and for providing specified services with the assets; in return, the concessionaire receives specified revenues from the operation of the assets; the assets revert to the public sector at expiration of the contract.

CONCHOIDAL FRACTURE Rupture of metal in which the fractured surface has a shell-like appearance.

CONFERENCE An affiliation of ship owners or operators over the same regional route(s) who agree to charge uniform rates, sailing schedules and other terms of carriage. A conference is 'closed' if one can enter only by the consent of existing members of the conference. It is 'open' if anyone can enter by meeting certain technical and financial standards. Conference members are common carriers.

CONGESTIONS Port/berth delays.

CONSERVANCY In some countries this fee is levied to retain upkeep of the approaches to waterways and canals.

CONSIGNEE The person to whom cargo is consigned as stated on the bill of lading.

CONSIGNOR The person named in the bill of lading as the one from whom the goods have been received for shipment.

CONSOLIDATION Cargo containing shipments of two or more shippers or suppliers. Container load shipments may be consolidated for one or more consignees.

CONSTRUCTION UNIT Unit equipped to assist during offshore construction and maintenance work.

CONSTRUCTIVE TOTAL LOSS When the cost of rescuing, reconditioning, handling and/or forwarding the goods to destination would exceed their value on arrival. When the repair of damage sustained by a vessel would cost more than the vessel would be worth after being repaired.

CONSUL Commercial representative of a country residing officially in another, whose duties facilitate business and represent the merchants of his nation.

CONSULAGE Duty paid to a consul for protection of goods.

CONSULAR FEE The privileged fees or perquisites charged by a consul for his official certificates and notarial legalizations.

CONSULAR INVOICE Form obtained from a consul on which a description of goods shipped is given in order that the proper duties may be levied when the goods are landed.

CONTAINER A van, flat rack, open top trailer or other similar trailer body onto or into which cargo is loaded and transported without chassis aboard ocean vessels; a large rectangular or square container/box of a strong structure that can withstand continuous rough handling from ship to shore and back. It opens from one side to allow cargo to be stacked and stowed into it. Containers may be ventilated, insulated, refrigerated, flat rack, vehicle rack, open top, bulk liquid, dry bulk or other configuration. Typical containers may be 20 feet, 40 feet, 45 feet or 53 feet in length, 8 feet or 8.6 feet in width and 8.6 feet or 9.6 feet in height.

CONTAINER FREIGHT STATION, CFS Shipping dock where cargo is loaded (stuffed) in, or unloaded (stripped or un-stuffed) from containers.

CONTAINER POOL Agreement between parties that allows the efficient use and supply of containers; a common supply of containers available to the shipper as required.

CONTAINER SHIP A ship constructed in such a way that containers can be easily stacked near and on top of each other under as well as on deck. A vessel designed to carry standard inter-modal containers, enabling efficient loading, unloading and transport to and from the vessel. Ocean-going merchant vessel designed to transport a unit load of standard-sized containers 8 feet square and 20 or 40 feet long. The hull is divided into cells that are easily accessible through large hatches and more containers can be loaded on deck atop the closed hatches. Loading and unloading can proceed simultaneously using giant travelling cranes at special berths. Container ships usually carry in the range of 25,000 to 70,000 deadweight tons. Whereas a general-cargo ship may spend as much as 70% of its life in port loading and discharging cargo, a container ship can be turned around in 24 hours or less, spending as little as 20% of its time in port. Specialized types of container ships can have a height of 8 feet, 8.6, 9 or 9.6 feet. Others are the LASH and SeaBee which carry floating containers (or 'lighters') and Ro/Ro ships, which may carry containers on truck trailers.

CONTAINER TERMINAL Area designed for stowage of cargo in containers or for empty containers, usually accessible by truck, rail and marine transportation, where containers are picked up, dropped off, maintained and stored.

CONTAINER YARD Material handling/storage facility used for completely unitized loads in containers and/or empty containers.

CONT (BH) Continent, Bordeaux – Hamburg range.

CONTRABAND Goods imported or exported contrary to law or proclamation; smuggled goods.

CONTRABAND OF WAR Anything (especially arms, stores or other things available for hostile purposes) forbidden to be supplied by neutrals to belligerents in time of war and liable to be captured and confiscated.

CONTRACT CARRIER Any person not a common carrier who, under special and individual contracts or agreements, transports passengers or cargo for compensation.

CONTRACT OF AFFREIGHTMENT, COA A service contract under which a ship owner agrees to transport a specified quantity of fuel products or specialty products, at a specified rate per ton, between designated loading and discharge ports. This type contract differs from a spot or consecutive voyage charter in that no particular vessel is specified.

CONTROLLED ATMOSPHERE Sophisticated, computer controlled systems that manage the mixture of gasses within a container throughout an individual journey, thereby reducing decay.

COP Custom Of the Port. Chartering term. Operations which take the peculiarities of the port/country into account.

CORIANDER An unbelliferous annual plant grown for its pungent fruit, used as a seasoning in India and for the essential oil expressed from its seeds.

COTTON SEED This is crushed to obtain the oil and the seed residue makes oilcake and meal for cattle food.

COW Crude Oil Washing. Washing of the oil tank with jets of the same oil. This is to replace washing with water which carries a risk of explosion and the problem of the disposal of cleaning water.

C/P Charter Party.

CPD Charterers' Paid Dues.

CPI Consumer Price Index.

CQD Customary Quick Dispatch.

CR *1* Credit or creditor. One to whom value is owed. *2* Current Rate.

CREDITOR One to whom value is owed.

CREW The personnel engaged on board ship, excluding the Master and Officers and the passengers on passenger ships.

CREW LIST List prepared by the Master of a ship, showing the full names, nationality, passport or discharge book number, rank and age of every Officer and crew member engaged on board that ship. This serves as one of the essential ship's documents which is always requested to be presented and handed over to the customs and immigration authorities when they board the vessel on arrival.

CRITICAL SPEED Revolution of Propeller per Minute (RPM) which is close to vibration rate of the engine. The speed corresponding to the RPM cannot be maintained at all times.

CROSS-TRADES Foreign-to-foreign trade carried

by ships from a nation other than the two trading nations.

CRUDE OIL WASHING A technique of cleaning tanks in oil tankers. *See also COW.*

CS Cotton Seed or Cases.

CTC Corn Trade Clauses.

CTL Constructive Total Loss. After an incident such as collision, grounding or fire, if it is too expensive to repair the ship, the insurer considers it is lost. The vessel is abandoned or sold as scrap.

CTLO Constructive Total Loss Only.

CUBIC CAPACITY The most important commercial measurement when the intrinsic weight of the cargo is so low that the ship becomes full without being loaded to the cargo line. Is expressed in cubic metres or cubic feet.

CURRENCY OF A BILL The period of time which must be elapsed before it is due to be paid.

CUSTOM HOUSE The place where duties imposed by the Government on imports and exports are collected.

CUSTOM OF MARKET This is binding on a person who deals in the market whether he knows it or not.

CUSTOMS BROKER Person or firm, licensed by customs authority of his country when required, engaged in entering and clearing goods through customs for a client (importer).

CUT-OFF TIME, CLOSING TIME Latest time a container may be delivered to a terminal for loading to a scheduled vessel, train or truck.

CWO Cash With Order.

D

D for DELTA   Morse = (– . .)

Flag = blue central horizontal stripe with smaller yellow strip above and below. When hoisted singly from a ship it means 'I am manœuvring with difficulty'. (Similar fog signal.)

DA Documents against Acceptance (insurance).

D/A CLAUSE Vessel must Discharge Afloat.

DAILY RUNNING COST Cost per day of operating a ship.

DANGEROUS CARGO All substances of an

inflammable or corrosive nature which are liable to spontaneous combustion either in themselves or when stowed adjacent to other substances and, when mixed with air, are liable to generate explosive gases or produce suffocation or poisoning or tainting of foodstuffs.

DANGEROUS LIQUIDS Liquids giving off inflammable vapour or corrosive substance.

DAUGHTER COMPASS Compass linked to the main (mother) gyroscopic compass giving the same indications and used for coastal navigation or compass correction calculations.

DAVITS Two radial arms (cranes) on a ship which hold the lifeboats. They are constructed to lower and lift the lifeboats the easiest way possible and must always lie unobstructed in case of an emergency.

DBB Deals, Battens and Boards.

D/C Deviation Clause (Insurance).

DD *1* Delivered.

2 Dry Dock. An enclosed basin into which a ship is taken for underwater cleaning and repairing. It is fitted with water tight entrance gates which, when closed, permit the dock to be pumped dry. Every two or three years the ship has to be put in a dry dock in order to check all the submerged parts, repaint them and eventually remove the propeller and the tail shaft.

D/D Days after Date.

DDO Damage Discharging Only.

DEADFREIGHT Space booked by shipper or charterer on a vessel but not used.

DEADFREIGHT FACTOR Percentage of a ship's carrying capacity that is not utilized.

DEAD RECKONING The finding of a vessel's position from course steered and distance run from starting point, without any observation of the sun or the stars. The term is supposed to have originated from the fact that the abbreviation 'ded' was used in ancient logbooks for the word 'deduced' and that it has been corrupted to 'dead'.

DEADWEIGHT, DWAT, DWCC A common measure of ship carrying capacity, the number of tons of cargo, stores and bunkers that a vessel can transport. It is the difference between the number of tons of water a vessel displaces 'light' and the number of tons it displaces 'when submerged to the "deep load line"'. A vessel's cargo capacity is less than its total deadweight tonnage. The difference in weight between a vessel when it is fully loaded and when it is empty (in general transportation terms, the 'net' meaning with fuel and stores on board without any cargo) measured by the water it displaces. This is the most common and useful measurement for shipping as it measures cargo capacity.

DEAD WORK The topside of a vessel, ie that portion of the hull above the waterline when the vessel is laden.

DECCA Navigation device whereby the position of a ship can be obtained via radio signals.

DECK GANG The Officers and seamen comprising the deck department aboard ship. Also called deck crew, deck department or just deck.

DECKHAND Seaman who works on the deck of a ship and remains in the wheelhouse attending to the orders of the Duty Officers during navigation and manœuvring. He also comes under the direct orders of the boatswain (bosun).

DECK HOUSE, mostly called WHEEL HOUSE Superstructure on the top deck of a vessel which contains the helm and other navigational instruments.

DECK LOG Also called Captain's Log or Logbook. A full nautical record of a ship's voyage, written up at the end of each watch by the Deck Officer on watch. The principal entries are courses steered, distance run, compass variations, sea and weather conditions, ship's position, principal headlands passed, names of lookouts, any unusual position and any unusual happenings such as fire, collision and the like.

DECK OFFICER As distinguished from Engineer Officer, refers to all Officers who assist the Master in navigating the vessel when at sea and supervise the handling of cargo when in port. Deck Officers are the Captain, First Officer also called Chief Mate, Second, Third, Fourth Officer or Mate and Cadets (apprentice Deck Officers).

DECONSOLIDATION POINT Place where loose or other non-containerized cargo is ungrouped for delivery.

DEEP SEA TRADES The traffic routes of both cargo and passenger vessels that are regularly engaged on the high seas or on long voyages.

DEEP STOWAGE Any bulk, bagged or other type of cargo stowed in single hold ships.

DEEPTANKS Tanks built on board vessels next to the normal dry cargo holds for transport of liquids such as vegetable oils (palm-oil, palm-kernel oil, cotton seed oil or linseed oil or latex.

DELD Delivered.

DEMDES Demurrage/Despatch money. Brokerage abbreviation of chartering terms. Amount to be paid if the ship is loading/discharging slower/faster than foreseen. Usually the Despatch money, which is paid by the ship owner, is half the amount of the Demurrage, which is paid by the Charterer.

DEMISE CHARTER *See Bare boat charter.*

DEMURRAGE A fee levied by the shipping company upon the port or supplier for not loading or unloading the vessel by a specified date agreed upon by contract. Usually, assessed upon a daily basis after the deadline. Time agreed is termed 'lay days'.

DERELICT Goods cast away or abandoned on account of wreck or other cause. An abandoned vessel.

DESPATCH Time saved, reward for quick turnaround. Opposite of demurrage. In dry cargo only.

DETENTION Where demurrage is to be paid for an agreed upon number of days any further delay is termed 'detention' in respect of which the ship owner can claim liquidated damages.

DEVIATION *1* Vessel deviation from specified voyage course. This may result in the release of an underwriter from his risk unless specially covered. The institute cargo clauses cover this at a premium to be arranged. To seek a port of refuge, if in the judgement of the Master the safety or best interest of the ship, crew or cargo requires it, when a ship is un-seaworthy from unfitness of structure, is not a deviation. If, however, the circumstances under which the ship leaves port are such that she will be compelled to deviate due to a shortage of fuel, the deviation is voluntary. Deviation may also preclude a ship owner from relying on any protecting clauses in his bills of lading, the effect being that he will be liable to the cargo owner as a common carrier.
2 Error caused to the magnetic compass by the influence of the steel of the ship and/or cargo.

DF Direction Finder. Used for locating the position of the ship by audio signals (not very accurate).

DGD Dangerous Goods Declaration.

DGL Dangerous Goods List.

DGRd Dangerous Goods Record.

DGRr Dangerous Goods Register.

DIRECTION, SET of the WIND, CURRENT These are opposite terms; the direction of the winds and waves being named from the point of compass from whence they come. The direction of the current is the point towards which it flows.

DIRTY MONEY Extra payment made to labourers for handling goods of an objectionable nature.

DISABLED SHIP When a ship is unable to sail efficiently or in a seaworthy state as a result of engine trouble, lack of Officers or crew, damage to the hull or ship's gear.

DISCHARGES An essential document for Officers and seamen as it serves as an official certificate confirming sea experience in the employment for which they were engaged.

DISCHARGE (US/OPA 90) Any emission (other than natural seepage), intentional or unintentional, and includes, but is not limited to, spilling, leaking, pumping, pouring, emitting, emptying or dumping.

DISPATCH MONEY A bonus paid by ship owners to charterers for discharging or loading a vessel in less time then stipulated in the charter party.

DISPLACEMENT The volume of water displaced by the ship, varies according to empty or loaded condition, a ton of displacement being 20 cwt. A displacement ton is estimated at 35 cubic feet of sea water or 36 cubic feet of fresh water.

DISTANCES, SPEED at SEA Distances at sea are measured in nautical miles of 6080ft (1852m) and speed in knots or miles per hour.

DNV Det Norske Veritas classification AS. Norwegian Classification Society.

DO Diesel Oil. Mainly used to run the auxiliary engines/alternator which provide the electrical power. On many large ships it is used in the main engine during the manœuvres (berthing/sailing). When the main engine is stopped for a long time it is better, and on some ships imperative, to have DO in all the system.

DOC Document Of Compliance (ISM Code). Certificate provided by the Administration stating that the owner/management complies with the ISM Code.

DOCK For ships, a cargo handling area parallel to the shoreline.

DOD Department Of Defence.

DOE Department of Energy.

DOLPHIN A block of wood with a ring bolt at each end for vessels to ride by; a mooring buoy. A mooring post or bollard placed at the entrance of a dock or on a quay, wharf or beach to make hawsers fast to.

DOMESTIC OFFSHORE TRADES Domestic shipping routes serving Alaska and non-continental US states and territories.

DONKEY ENGINE Auxiliary engine for duties independent of a vessel's propelling engines.

DOP, DOSP Dropping Outward (Sea) Pilot (time). When the vessel leaves the last discharge port. It is often the time accepted as the end of a voyage charter.

DOT Department of Transportation.

DOUBLE BOTTOM General term for all watertight spaces contained between the outside bottom plating, the tank top and the margin plate. The double bottoms are sub-divided into a number of separate tanks which may contain boiler feed water, drinking water, fuel oil, ballast etc.

DOUGHNUT HOLES In Alaska these are water areas inside the chain of outer islands which are classified as 'international waters' because they are further than 3 miles or 12 miles from any shore line but they are entirely surrounded by US territorial waters (Lloyd's List A-52). Some ships are taking advantage of this legal trick to get rid of waste which otherwise has to be dumped at sea at the same distance from shore. For many purposes the US uses the 3 miles limit for its territorial waters so that Doughnut Holes can also be found on the Gulf of Mexico coast.

DP Designated Person. For the ISM Code, any member of the owner's staff who is aware of the problems of the vessels and who has direct access to the top management.

DRAUGHT The depth of a ship in the water. The vertical distance between the waterline and the keel, in the US expressed in feet, elsewhere in metres.

DREDGING Removal of sediment to deepen access channels, provide turning basins for ships and adequate water depth along waterside facilities.

DRILLING UNIT Fitted with drilling rig (oil derrick with rotary drill and mud pumping system), drilling for petroleum.

DRILL SHIP Regular ship shaped vessel, production ship. Positioned by anchors or dynamic positioning. Has its own propulsion machinery.

DRY BULK Low density cargo, such as agri-food products, fertilizers and ores that are transported in bulk carriers.

DRY CARGO Merchandise other than liquid.

DRY CARGO SHIP Vessel which carries all merchandise. Some dry cargo ships may also have some compartments of the hold as tanks destined for the transport of liquids in bulk (tallow, vegetable oils, cotton seed oil etc).

D/S Days after Sight.

DSC Digital Selective Calling. GMDSS System: MF/HF/VHF facility which allows automatic access to coast stations equipped with the system. A short list is available to select quickly the nature of distress; unfortunately 'pirate attack' has been forgotten although it is one which needs maximum automation and discretion.

DT Deep Tank.

DTBA Date To Be Agreed. Date To Be Advized.

DUAL PURPOSE SHIP Specially constructed ship able to carry different types of cargoes such as ore and/or oil.

DUC D'ALBE A mooring pile. Named after the Flanders duke who is said to have invented this type of potential execution by tying a person to a pole at low tide to give him time to change his mind on his choice of religion.

DUFF Coal dust or small coals after separation of nuts.

DUMB BARGE Barge without sails or motive power.

DUNNAGE A term applied to loose wood or other material used in a ship's hold for the protection or secure stowage of cargo. Consists of wood, mats, bamboo.

DWT, DWCC Deadweight Tons, Dead Weight Cargo Capacity. Weights of the cargo which can be lifted, usually expressed in metric or long tons. Not to be confused with the deadweight itself which includes many other weights: bunkers, fresh water, provisions, stores, ballast, constant. They can add up to a few thousands tons on a Panamax bulker.

DWAT Dead Weight All Told.

E

E for ECHO　　　**Morse = (.)**

Flag = Blue over red. When hoisted singly from a ship it means 'I am altering my course to starboard'.

E&EL Each and Every Loss.

E&OE Errors & Omissions Excepted (*such as this list.*)

EBB TIDE The receding or running out of the sea.

ECDIS Electronic Chart Display and Information System. Based on vectorial representation of features, this system is the best available as it can be coupled to many other devices. Unfortunately, since the availability of GPS positioning much hydrographical information has been found to be out of position by several miles at times (eg Providence Channel in the Bahamas), therefore many charts must be redrawn. It is only with these charts that electronic facilities, such as automatic alarms for shallow water, can be connected.

ECOSOC ECOnomic & SOcial Council of the United Nations. UN agency parenting the IAEA (International Atomic Energy Agency), the ICAO (International Civil Aviation Organisation) and the IMO.

ECSA European Community Shipowners Associations. Represents the interests of European ship owners at EU level. Its membership comprises the national ship owners associations of the EU and Norway.

ECUK East Coast of the United Kingdom.

ECV Each Cargo Voyage.

EDI Electronic Data Interchange.

EDIFACT Electronic Data Interchange For Administration, Commerce and Trade (sponsored by United Nations).

EE Errors Excepted.

EEC European Economic Community.

EFFECTIVE HORSEPOWER The actual power produced by the engine to propel a vessel.

EFTA European Free Trade Association.

EMBARGO An order of prohibition on trade or shipping issued by a government. Government prohibition against the sailing of a vessel from port. Period before a document or information can be disclosed.

EMINENT DOMAIN Sovereign power to take property for necessary public use, with reasonable compensation.

EML Estimated Maximum Loss.

EMS *1* Emergency Schedule IMO/IMDG Code. Emergency Procedures for Ships Carrying Dangerous Goods.
2 Environmental Management System. ISO Standard.

ENTREPOT (French) A warehouse, distribution depot, bonded warehouse.

ENTRY, ENTRY OUT A customs form used for the clearance of ships or merchandise.

EOHP Except Otherwise Herein Provided.

EP Entry Permit.

EPIRB Emergency Position Indicating Radio Beacon. Small buoyant transmitter which should always remain afloat if the ship sinks and automatically send a distress message via satellites.

EQUASIS European ship and operator information system which became operational in May 2000. Based on a French system, it is an important tool for anybody with an interest in or responsibility for maritime safety, to select ships of high quality, and also an useful tool for PSC inspectors (Commission of the European Communities). It will be really efficient when seafarers can rely on it for a good idea of the effective seaworthiness of the vessel to which they are sent by crewing agencies.

ESC European Shippers Council. Represents the interests of shippers represented by 12 national transport user organizations and a number of key European commodity trade associations.

ESPARTO A strong kind of grass which is baled and exported from North Africa. Used for the production of paper.

ESPO European Sea Ports Organisation. Represents the common interests of more than 800 seaports in the European Union and neighbouring countries. Its membership consists of port authorities, port administrations and port associations.

ETA Estimated Time of Arrival. Some agents assume it is the Expected Time of Arrival or even the Exact Time of Arrival, so they are upset when the ship cannot keep the schedule. At times they require the 'Earliest ETA', which is more reasonable. This time must be transmitted quite often to other services. *See also Pilotage and VTS.*

ETC Estimated Time of Completion. Estimated time of completion of the cargo operations. Normally the agent should ask the captain how long he requires to make the ship seaworthy after the ETC. Very few agents adhere to this, order the pilot and the tugs for the ETC and have to pay huge waiting times to these services if the ship needs more time to be ready.

ETD Estimated Time of Departure. Estimated time of departure of the vessel. Does not necessarily coincide with the time of completion for the reasons mentioned above, or because the ship has to wait for another reason: tide, daylight etc.

ETR Estimated Time of Readiness. Time at which the ship will be ready to load, for instance when the crew has to clean the holds first.

ETS Expected Time of Sailing.

EUSC Effective US Control.

EVEN KEEL When the draft of a ship is the same fore and aft.

EXCAVATOR *See Backhoe.*

EXIMBANK Export-Import Bank. A Federal agency that aids in financing exports of US goods and services through direct loans, loan guarantee, and insurance.

F

F for FOXTROT   Morse = (. . – .)

Flag = red diamond on white background. When hoisted singly from a ship it means 'I am disabled. Communicate with me'.

F1B Radio transmission designator. Telegraphy using frequency modulation = Narrow-Band Direct-Printing (Telex) (ALRS).

F1D Radio transmission designator. Data transmission using frequency modulation, with a single channel containing quantized or digital information without the use of a modulating sub-carrier (ALRS).

F2B Radio transmission designator. Telegraphy using frequency modulation, with a single channel containing quantified or digital information with the use of a modulating sub-carrier for automatic reception (ALRS).

F2C Radio transmission designator. Facsimile transmission using frequency modulation with a single channel containing quantified or digital information with the use of a modulating sub-carrier (ALRS).

F2D Radio transmission designator. Data transmission using frequency modulation, with a single channel containing quantified or digital information with the use of a modulating sub-carrier (ALRS).

F3C Radio transmission designator. Facsimile transmission using frequency modulation with a single channel containing analogue information (ALRS).

F3E Radio transmission designator. Telephony using frequency modulation (ALRS).

FA Free Alongside.

FAA Free of All Average (in insurance for hull policies).

FAC Fast As Can.

FACS Federation of American Controlled Shipping.

FAIR (Shipbuilding) Denotes evenness or regularity of a curve or line.

FAIT ACCOMPLI (French) An accomplished fact, something already done.

F&D Freight and Demurrage.

FAQ Fair Average Quality.

FARINA Flour or potato starch.

FAS Free Along Side (of ship).

FC&S Free of Capture and Seizure. Insurance term. Used until 1982 in all marine insurance contracts to refer to the war exclusion clause. Discontinued in the UK cargo insurance market in 1982 and in the hull insurance market in 1983 (BIMCO).

FCC First Class Charterers.

FCL Full Container Load.

FEDERAL MARITIME COMMISSION (FMC) Authorized tariffs and rate-making procedures on conferences operating in the United States.

FEEDER *1* A grain container or reservoir constructed around the hatchway between two decks of a ship which, when filled with grain, automatically feeds or fills in the vacant areas in the lower holds.

2 Name of a ship bringing or taking containers to port for on-carriage to another destination.

FENDER Lengths of spars tight together or other material (rubber tyres) hung over the side of a vessel to avoid chafing alongside the wharf.

FEPORT Federation of European Private Port Operators. It unites national and regional representative associations of private port operators in the EU as well as individual stevedoring companies and terminal operators.

FEU Forty Foot Equivalent Unit (containers).

FFA Free From Alongside. The seller pays lighterage charges in the port of destination.

FHEX Fridays, Holidays Excluded.

FHINC Fridays, Holidays Included.

FIO Free In and Out.

FIOS(T) Free In and Out, Stowed (and Trimmed).

FIREMAN An unlicensed member of the engine room staff whose duties consist of standing watch in the boiler room and insuring the oil burning equipment is working properly.

FIRST REFUSAL First attempt at best offer that can be matched.

FITTING OUT The act of equipping a vessel so that she is in a proper condition for the voyage.

FIXED COSTS Costs that do not vary with the level of activity. Some fixed costs continue even if no cargo is carried, for instance terminal leases, rent, property tax.

FIXED JIB Crane whereby the jib always stays at the same angle and cannot reach out further.

FIXTURE Conclusion of shipbrokers' negotiations to charter a ship, an agreement.

FLAG OF CONVENIENCE (FOC) The registration of ships in a country where tax on the profit of trading ships is low or where requirements concerning manning or maintenance are not stringent. Sometimes referred to as flags of necessity; denotes registration of vessels in foreign nations that offer favourable tax structures and regulations; also the flag representing the nation under whose jurisdiction a ship is registered. Ships are always registered under the laws of one nation but are not always required to establish their home location in that country. Country of registry representing the legal system under which the ship is managed but not the nationality of the owner, management, crew. Some FOCs are tiny countries with a few thousands inhabitants (St Vincent & Grenadines, Cayman Islands, Nauru); others are landlocked (Luxembourg) and do not have a real maritime administration. They often delegate their obligations to other services: Classes, agencies etc.

FLAX A fibre obtained from the stems of a plant. Used in the production of linen.

FLG, FLAG Broker abbreviation indicating the country in which the vessel is registered. *See also Flag of convenience.*

FLNG Floating Liquid Natural Gas unit.

FLOATING OIL STORAGE Oil stored on floating vessels. It has been the practice for oil to be stored in large laid-up oil tankers in order to offset the loss involved while the tankers are inactive.

FLOATING POLICY *See Open policy.*

FLOORINGS Wood, planed boards from 0.5 to 1.5

inches thick and 4 to 4.5 inches broad, average length 15 to 17 feet.

FLOTSAM, JETSAM Jetsam is the part of a shipwreck that has been thrown overboard (*see jettison*). Flotsam is what floated off on its own accord. Wreckage found attached to a buoy is *lagan*. In early days flotsam went to the crown and jetsam to the lord of the manor on whose land it washed up.

FLUORSPAR or FLUORITE A mineral found in limestone districts, used as a flux in the reduction of metallic ores, also in the manufacture of pottery.

FLUVIO-MARITIME BARGE Barge constructed with a higher freeboard, allowing it to go out at sea within limits. Some are for dry cargo, others for liquids.

FMC Federal Maritime Commission.

FO Free Out. For Orders. Fuel Oil, fuel mainly used for propulsion but also with some auxiliary engines. IFO = Intermediary FO, HFO = Heavy FO.

FOB Free On Board. Cost of a product before transportation and loading aboard costs are added in. Export term in which the price quoted by the exporter does not include the costs of ocean transportation but does include loading on board the vessel. The goods are then at the risk of the purchaser, who is liable for freight. Exception: in the port of Antwerp FOB means only alongside of the ship.

FOD Free Of Damage.

FONASBA Federation of National Association of Shipbrokers and Agents.

FOQ Free On Quay.

FOOT = 12 inches, 0.3048 metres.

FOR Free On Rail.

FORCE MAJEURE Clause limiting responsibilities of charterers, shippers and receiver of cargo in case of severe and unforeseeable damage such as earthquakes, floods. *See also Act of God.*

FORE & AFT From end to end of the vessel.

FORECASTLE Also known as fo'csle . The raised part of the forward end of a ship's hull. The inside space may be used for crew accommodation or quarters, though on new ships this space is being used for the storage of paints, tackle, deck and engine stores, tarpaulins etc.

FOREIGN TRADE ZONE A free port in a country divorced from customs authority but under government control. Merchandise, except contraband, may be stored in the zone without being subject to import duty regulations. Manufacturing can also take place in this area.

FOREPEAK Enclosed part of the forward part of the vessel used for storekeeping or as a tank usually used for drinking water.

FORKLIFT Vehicle built to transport cargo on forks in the front. Capacities vary from 1 to 50 tons.

FORWARD At or in the direction of the bow. Also the fore part of the ship.

FORWARDING & SHIPPING AGENT One whose business it is to combine the various sections of transport into one whole, to see that the links of the chain – road, railway, cartage, dock charges, insurance and freight – are economically combined and interwoven so that the merchant or shipper has the fullest advantage of the lowest rates.

FOURHOOK Ring with four chains with hooks attached in order to lift stevedore pallets.

FOYBOAT A boat employed to assist in mooring and unmooring ships (NE coast of England).

FPSO Floating Production Storage and Offloading vessel. Large tanker, often without propulsion of her own, staying in a fixed position to process and store oil awaiting to be loaded on another vessel. In July 1999 the largest one was the *Girassol*, built by Hyundai for the service of ELF in Angola from 2001. She has a storage capacity of 2m barrels and a process capacity of 200,000 barrels a day.

FPT Fore Peak Tank.

FRAME Strengthening beam at regular distances along the inside of the hull plating.

FR&CC Free of Riots and Civil Commotions.

FREE ALONGSIDE Price includes delivery alongside the vessel without extra cost to the buyer.

FREE DELIVERY Shipper or vendor is bound to deliver the goods at a specific place free of cost. Usually the term does not include customs duties.

FREE IN and OUT Cargo to be loaded and discharged free of charge to vessel. Vessel only paying actual port charges.

FREE LIFT Attachment of a forklift truck whereby the mast is designed in such a way that when the load is raised the mast does not get any higher.

FREE PRATIQUE Clearance by the health authorities. Yellow flag = request free pratique = 'I have not had any contagious diseases on board in the last 48 hours.'

FREE SURFACE The surface that is not restricted by any means within the tanks of a ship.

FREE TRADE ZONE Zone often within a port (but not always so located) designated by government of a country for duty-free entry of any non-prohibited goods. Merchandise may be stored, displayed, used for manufacturing etc within the zone and re-exported without duties being levied. Also referred to as free port.

FREIGHT Cargo transported on board ship.

FREIGHT CARCASS (New Zealand) Equals 60 pounds weight of meat.

FREIGHT FORWARDER Arranges shipments for customers by reserving space on board ship, preparing documents for shipment and clearing by customs. Does not actually carry the cargo or conduct business for the ship.

FREIGHT PAYABLE AT DESTINATION Method of paying the freight often used for shipment of bulk cargo where weight is established on discharge from the ship.

FREIGHT RATE The charge made for the transportation of freight. Money payable on delivery of cargo in a mercantile condition and covering the transport cost by sea.

FREIGHT TON 1 ton = 1 cubic metre = one freight ton. 1 ton = 2 cubic metres = two freight tons. In freight calculation the expression is 'weight or measurement, whichever is the greater'. Also 40 cubic feet for merchandise, 42 cubic feet for timber.

FRUSTRATION Charterers when cancelling agreements sometimes quote 'doctrine of frustration', ie when a vessel is lost or extensively delayed.

FSA Formal Safety Assessment. Study of risks which should improve the design of ships and also their actual maintenance.

FSW Frisian Shipyard Welgelegen (Netherlands).

FTRR&I For Their Respective Rights and Interests.

FULLER'S EARTH A variety of clay consisting of hydrous bisilicate of alumina with an added mixture of iron, magnesia and other salts.

FUTURES Contracts for goods and stocks sold for delivery at a future date.

FW Fresh Water. Can designate either:
1 Fresh water used by the ship for drinking, cooling system of engine, showers, toilet etc. Previously the amount was the biggest on departure in order to

safely reach the port of destination. Nowadays most ships produce their own fresh water in an 'evaporator' fed with sea water and using the heat of the engine. Often 25 tons a day are made; some 10 tons are used so that 15 tons can be added to the stock with the result that the ship arrives with full tanks. This added weight is generally compensated by the consumption of FO and DO.

2 Fresh Water as opposed to Sea Water regarding the density of the water supporting the ship. Normally the density of SW is 1.000 but in places like the Panama canal it can be 0.985 because it is warmer.

FWAD Fresh Water Arrival Draught.

FWD Fresh Water Damage.

FXX Radio transmission designator. Frequency modulation of main carrier other than F1B, F3E and frequency modulation facsimile (ALRS).

G

●●●●●●●●●●●●●●●●●●●●●●●●●●●●●●●

G for GOLF   **Morse = (– – .)**

Flag = six yellow and blue vertical bars. When hoisted singly from a ship it means 'I require a pilot'. Still widely used.

●●●●●●●●●●●●●●●●●●●●●●●●●●●●●●●

G1D Radio transmission designator. Phase modulation with a single channel containing quantified or digital information without the use of a modulating sub-carrier for data transmission (ALRS).

G2B Radio transmission designator. Phase modulation (automatic reception). A single channel containing quantified or digital information with the use of a modulating sub-carrier (ALRS).

GA General Average. The cost incurred to bring the ship out of a dangerous position must be shared by all the parties interested in the rescue, which means also the cargo owners. These are then required to contribute to a General Average. This is quite easy with a bulker, having one parcel of cargo, but a nightmare with a container vessel where thousands of parcels with different B/Ls are stowed in the containers.

G/A CON General Average Contribution.

G/A DEP General Average Deposit.

GANGWAY A narrow portable platform or steps used as a passage, by persons entering or leaving a vessel moored alongside a pier or quay.

GANTRY CRANE Crane or hoisting device moored on a frame or structure spanning an intervening space and designed to hoist containers into or out of a ship.

GAS FREEING The introduction of fresh air into a tank with the object of removing toxic, flammable and inert gasses and increasing the oxygen content to 21% by volume.

GAS TANKER Specially designed for the transport of condensed (liquefied) gases. The most important gases are ammonia, ethylene, LNG (Liquefied Natural Gas) which consists mainly of methane and is cooled to a temperature of minus 163 degrees Celsius and LPG (Liquefied Petroleum Gas) such as butane or propane.

GATEWAY A point at which freight moving from one territory to another is interchanged between transportation lines.

GATT General Agreements on Tariffs and Trade (Geneva 1947).

GCBS General Council of British Shipping.

GCN Gross Commission N. Broker abbreviation regarding their commission. (GCN 3.75%.)

GCN GENCON Type of charter party.

GDP Gross Domestic Product. The total value of goods and services produced by a nation over a given period, usually 1 year.

GENERAL AVERAGE Where any extraordinary sacrifice or expenditure is voluntary and reasonably made or incurred, in time of peril, for the purpose of preserving the property imperilled in the common adventure and this act has resulted in success, then the loss comes within general average and must be borne proportionally by all who are interested, ie vessel, freight and cargo.

GENERAL AVERAGE CLAIMS The onus of proof is upon the party claiming general average to show the loss or expenditure claimed is properly allowable as general average.

GENERAL CARGO A non-bulk cargo composed of miscellaneous goods, cases, bundles of steel, crates, bags etc.

GEOGRAPHICAL ROTATION Ports in order of calling.

GESAMP Joint Group of Experts on the Scientific Aspects of Marine environmental Protection.

GINSENG Root of a medicinal plant found in Korea, China, Nepal, Canada and eastern USA.

GL Germanischer Lloyd. German Classification Society.

GLONASS GLObal NAvigation Satellite System.

GLYCERINE A clear, colourless or pale yellow syrupy liquid derived from the saponification of fats and oils in the soap industry.

GM Distance between the centre of gravity and the meta-centre, the force that brings a ship back upright.

GMDSS Global Maritime Distress and Safety System. A radio communication system which takes advantage of latest technology to enhance safety and allow ships to sail without a Radio Officer. Implemented in 1992, it became fully operational on 1 February 1999. During this time it provoked thousands of false alarms and bulkers sank without any warning by their EPIRBs.

GMT Greenwich Mean Time. Now mostly replaced by UTC or Z.

GNP Gross National Product: GDP plus the net income accruing from foreign sources.

GODOWN The name given to warehouses in Africa and the Far East.

GOTHENBURG STANDARD A measurement of pit props and sleepers = 190 cubic feet or 5.097 cubic metres.

GOVERNMENT IMPELLED Cargo owned or subsidized by the Federal Government.

GPS Global Positioning System. US satellite based system that gives an accuracy of about 0.2 miles as the signal is variably distorted for military and security purposes. Local corrections are often provided through a DGPS system.

GRAIN CAPACITY Cubic capacity in grain.

GREAT LAKES PORTS Ports in the lakes of Canada and/or USA (popular for grain shipments). In Canada: Port Arthur and Fort William on Lake Superior and Hamilton, Kingston, Toronto and Prescott on Lake Ontario. In USA: Chicago, Detroit, Milwaukee on Lake Michigan, Duluth and Superior on Lake Superior and Toledo in Lake Erie.

GREAT LAKES SHIP Cargo ship developed to carry raw materials and manufactured goods on the Great Lakes. Most carry bulk cargoes of grain, iron ore or coal. The size of these vessels allows entrance to the locks giving access to the Lakes.

GROSS and NET TONNAGE, GT&NT Gross tonnage is the basis on which manning rules and safety regulations are applied and registration fees are reckoned. Port fees are also often reckoned on the basis of GT and NT. GT and NT are defined according to formulae which take into account, among other things, the volume of the vessel's enclosed spaces (GT) and the volume of its holds (NT). Expressed in tonnes of 100 cubic feet or 2.8317 (or Moorsom ton).

GROSS FREIGHT Freight money collected or to be collected without calculating the expenses relating to the running cost of the ship for the voyage undertaken.

GROSS REGISTERED TONS A common measurement of the internal volume of a ship with certain spaces excluded. One ton equals 100 cubic feet; the total of all the enclosed spaces within a ship expressed in tons, each of which is equivalent to 100 cubic feet. No more used. Measurement of commercial vessel based on the total volume occupied by enclosed spaces. One actual ton of measurement is the equivalent of 2.8317 cubic metres (Moorsom ton).

GROUNDAGE Money paid for permission to anchor.

GROUNDING Contact by a ship with the bottom while she is moored or anchored as a result of the water level dropping.

GROUND NUT Earth nut, *pistache de terre*, monkey nut, peanut, Manila nut. By expression these seeds yield a large quantity of oil. Cultivated in all tropical and sub-tropical areas. Groundnuts are ripened underground. Those having more then 8.5% of moisture are not suitable for shipment.

GROUPAGE The grouping together of several compatible consignments into a full container load. Also referred to as consolidation.

GSM Goods Sound Merchantable.

GUANO Seabird dung.

GYPSUM A soft mineral from which is manufactured plaster of Paris, also used as a fertilizer.

GYROSCOPIC COMPASS Compass based on the principle of the gyroscope whereby the true north-south axis is indicated, only varying with the geographical position on the globe.

H

H for Hotel   **Morse = (. . . .)**

Flag = vertically divided in two, white at the hoist, red at the fly. When hoisted singly from a ship it means 'I have a pilot on board'. Still widely used.

H2A Radio transmission designator. Telegraphy by the on-off keying of a tone modulated carrier, Morse code: single-sideband, full carrier (ALRS).

H2B Radio transmission designator. Selective calling signal using a single frequency code, single-sideband, full carrier (ALRS).

H3E Radio transmission designator. Telephony using amplitude modulation: single-sideband, full carrier (ALRS).

H9W Radio transmission designator. Composite emission: single-sideband, full carrier; composite system with one or more channels containing quantified or digital information together with one or more channels containing analogue information (eg combination of telegraphy and telephony). (ALRS).

HAEMATITE A valuable iron ore.

HAGUE RULES Code of minimum conditions for the carriage of cargo under a bill of lading.

HA OR D Havre, Antwerp or Dunkirk.

HARBOUR DUES, PORT DUES Various local charges against all seagoing vessels entering a harbour, to cover maintenance of channel depths, buoys, lights etc. Harbours do not necessarily have these charges.

HARBOUR MASTER A person usually having the experience of a certified master mariner and having a good knowledge of the characteristics of the port and its whole area. He administers the entire shipping movements that take place in and within reach of the port for which he is responsible.

HARD AGROUND A vessel which has gone aground and is incapable of re-floating under her own power.

HARD CURRENCY A currency which is sound enough to be accepted internationally and which is usually fully convertible.

HARTAL General stoppage of work (India).

HARTER ACT (1893) This US statute refers to merchandise or property transported from or between ports of the United States and foreign ports. Now partially superseded by the US Carriage of Goods by Sea Act of 1936.

HATCH An opening, generally rectangular, in a ship's deck, affording access to the compartment below.

HAWSE PIPES The pipes in the bow of a vessel through which the anchor cables pass.

HAWSER Large strong rope used for towing purposes and for securing or mooring ships. Hawsers are now mostly made of steel or a combination of steel and manila or polyester rope.

HAZMAT Hazardous Material.

HBL Hydrostatic Balanced Loading. Method of loading large oil tankers which extends the lives of tankers from 25 to 30 years with regard to MARPOL phase-out provision.

HC Held Covered.

HEAVY GRAIN Wheat, maize and rye.

HEAVY LIFT CHARGE A charge levied for lifting articles too heavy to be handled by normal lifting gear and whereby special lifting tackle or equipment is necessary.

HECTOPASCAL, hPa Unit of pressure used in weather reports and forecasts. Is equivalent to and replaces the millibar.

HELM A tiller or a wheel generally installed on the bridge or wheelhouse of a ship to turn the rudder during manœuvring and navigation. It is, in fact, the steering wheel of the ship.

HEMP A plant, the bark of which yields a fibre longer and stronger than flax. 1 ton (2240lbs) is estimated to measure 105 to 110 cubic feet. Used for making rope.

HF High Frequency. 3 – 30Mhz.

HH Havre to Hamburg (inclusive).

HHDW Handy, Heavy Deadweight (scrap).

HHP High Holding Power. Anchor type (NI).

HIDE Skin of any large or full grown animal such as horse, cow, ox, buffalo. Transported dry, raw, dressed or undressed or in layers with raw salt in between.

HIRE Time charter remuneration.

HMM Hyundai Merchant Marine. Korean shipping company.

HOGGED, HOGGING Implies that the two ends of a vessel's deck droop lower than the mid-ship part, consequently that her keel and bottom are so strained as to curve upwards. Opposite to sagging.

HOGSHEAD A liquid measure containing 63 old

wine gallons. Capacity of cask varying according to the contents and locality. A hogshead of beer is 54 gallons.

HOIST The action of lifting cargo.

HOISTING WIRE Special flexible wire rope for lifting purposes, generally being of six strands with 19 wires in each strand and in most cases having a hemp rope at the centre.

HOLD A general name for the spaces below the main deck designated for stowage of general cargo. A hold on a tanker is usually just forward of #1 cargo tank. Some newer tankers have no hold.

HORSEPOWER, hp A standard usually adopted for measuring mechanical power. The rate at which an engine works when it does 33,000 foot-pounds of work per minute, a foot-pound being the amount of work necessary to raise a weight of one pound through a foot.

HOVERCRAFT A vessel used for the transportation of passengers and cargo, riding on a cushion of air formed under it. It is very manœuvrable and is also amphibious.

HRA Human Reliability Analysis. Used in safety studies.

HSC High Speed Craft. Mostly ferries, catamaran, hovercraft etc.

HTC Highly Toxic Chemical (poison). A chemical falling within any of the following categories:

1 A chemical that has a median lethal dose (LD50) of 50 milligrams or less per kilogram of body weight when administered orally to albino rats weighing between 200 and 300 grams each.

2 A chemical that has a median lethal dose (LD50) of 200 milligrams or less per kilogram of body weight when administered by continuous contact for 24 hours (or less, if death occurs within 24 hours) with the bare skin of albino rabbits weighing between 2 and 3 kilograms each.

3 A chemical that has a median lethal concentration (LC50) of gas or vapour in air of 200 parts per million (ppm) or less by volume or 2 milligrams per litre or less of mist, fume or dust, when administered by continuous inhalation for 1 hour (or less, if death occurs within 1 hour) to albino rats weighing between 200 and 300 grams each, provided such concentration or condition or both is likely to be encountered by man when the chemical is used in any reasonably foreseeable manner.

4 A chemical that is a liquid having a saturated

vapour concentration (ppm) at 20°C equal to or greater than ten times its LC50 (vapour) value (ppm) if the LC50 value is 1000 parts per million (ppm) or less when administered by continuous inhalation for 1 hour to albino rats weighing between 200 and 300 grams each, provided such concentration or condition or both is likely to be encountered by man when the chemical is used in any reasonably foreseeable manner.

HULL Shell or body of a ship. The uppermost continuous deck having permanent means of closing all openings.

HW High Water.

HWM High Water Mark.

HWONT High Water On Neap Tide.

HWOST High Water Ordinary Spring Tide.

HYDROFOIL A craft lifting itself through speed out of the water onto ski-type protrusions and gliding over water, decreasing friction between the water and the hull.

I for India.   Morse = (. .)

Flag = black disk on yellow ground. When hoisted singly from a ship it means 'I am altering my course to port'.

IACS International Association of Classification Societies. Grouping of the main classification societies (about 10 in 1997) in order to raise the standards.

IADC International Association of Drilling Contractors.

IBC CODE International Bulk Chemical Code. Code for the construction and equipment of ships carrying dangerous chemicals in bulk as adopted by IMO/MEPC.19(22) for ships built after 1 July 1986. (Often wrongly defined in BA publications and charts as International Bulk Carrier code).

IBNR Incurred But Not Reported.

ICAS52 International Convention on the Arrest of Seagoing Ships 1952. Allows the creditor of shipping debts to present his claim in any country signatory of the convention and arrest the vessel if needed.

ICC International Chamber of Commerce.

ICCL International Council of Cruise Lines.

ICES International Council for the Exploration of the Sea.

ICS International Chamber of Shipping.

IFF Institute of Freight Forwarders.

IFO Intermediate Fuel Oil.

IFSMA International Federation of Ship Masters Association. Organization grouping all the national Masters associations, formed in 1974. Established in London. Over 8,000 shipmasters from more than 40 countries are affiliated to IFSMA. Was granted consultative status at IMO in 1975. Email: hq@ifsma.org. Website: www.ifsma.org.

IGC CODE International Gas Carrier Code. Code for the construction and equipment of ships carrying liquified gases in bulk.

IG(S) Inert Gas (System). Non reactive gas (nitrogen, CO_2) used to fill the tanks to prevent an accidental fire or explosion. A system of preventing any explosion in the cargo tanks of a tanker by replacing the cargo, as it is pumped out, by an inert gas. Gas-freeing must be carried out subsequently if workers have to enter the empty tanks.

IHO International Hydrographic Organization.

IHP Indicated Horse Power. The work of the steam on the cylinders without reference to resistance of the engine's friction etc.

ILDD In Lieu of Dry Dock. Class survey, mostly underwater, which allows the ship owner to postpone a dry docking.

ILF International Lifeboat Federation.

ILO International Labour Organization. Based in Geneva, it is one of the oldest components of the UN system of specialized agencies and has been involved over the years in appraising and seeking to improve and regulate conditions for seafarers. In its unusual tripartite way, involving official representatives of government, employer and employee interests, its joint Maritime Commission is looking at the employment of foreign seafarers with a view to implementing the application of minimum labour standards, on crew accommodation, accident prevention, medical examination and medical care, food and catering and Officers' competency.

IMDG International Maritime Dangerous Goods Code. One of the most important realizations of the IMO. The code defines most dangerous goods and provides directives for their carriage and segregation.

IMF International Monetary Fund.

IMLPA International Maritime Lecturers Association.

IMO International Maritime Organization: Formerly known as the Inter-Governmental Maritime Consultative Organization (IMCO), was established in 1948 through the United Nations to coordinate international maritime safety and related practices.

IMPA International Maritime Pilot's Association. Located in Belgium but mostly managed from the Netherlands.

IN BOND Cargo moving under customs control where duty has not yet been paid.

INDEMNITY Security for damage or loss. Compensation for loss or injury.

INDICATED HORSEPOWER The power without reference to resistance of the engine's friction etc.

INDUCEMENT Placing a port on a vessel's itinerary because the volume of cargo offered by that port justifies the cost of (re-)routing the vessel.

INERT CONDITION A condition in which the oxygen content throughout the atmosphere of the tank has been reduced to 8% or less by volume by addition of inert gas.

INERT GAS A gas or a mixture of gases, such as flue gas, containing insufficient oxygen to support the combustion of hydrocarbons. A mixture of nitrogen and CO_2. The inert gas takes the place of the explosive gases and prevents the air (with its oxygen content) penetrating tanks.

INERT GAS PLANT All equipment fitted to supply, cool, clean, pressurize, monitor and control delivery of inert gas to the tank system.

INERT GAS SYSTEM A plant and inert gas distribution system together with means for preventing backflow of cargo gases, fixed and portable measuring instruments and control devices.

INERTING The introduction of fresh air into a tank with the object of attaining the inert condition.

INF CODE International Code for the Safe Carriage of Packaged Irradiated Nuclear Fuel, Plutonium and High-Level Radioactive Wastes on board Ships.

INFLAMMABLE LIQUIDS Liquids liable to spontaneous combustion which give off inflammable vapours at or below 80°F. For example, ether, ethyl, benzine, gasoline, paints, enamels, carbon disulphide etc.

INHERENT VICE Defect or fault belonging to the nature of the article, which by its natural development can lead to its destruction.

INLAND CARRIER A transportation company that hauls export or import traffic between ports and inland points.

INLAND WATERS Term referring to lakes, streams, rivers, canals, waterways, inlets, bays etc.

INMARSAT International Maritime Satellite System for communication.

IN PERSONAM Legal action against a person.

IN REM Legal action against an object or the owner of it (eg a ship).

INST Instant. Present month.

INST CLAUSES Clauses officially accepted by the Institute of London Underwriters.

INSURABLE INTEREST The party effecting the insurance must be so situated with regard to the property insured as to expect pecuniary benefit from its safety and of pecuniary loss from its damage or destruction.

INSURANCE A contract whereby, for payment, called a premium, one party agrees to insure the other against loss or damage.

INTEGRATED TUG BARGE A large barge of about 600 feet and 22,000 tons cargo capacity, integrated from the rear on to the bow of a tug purposely constructed to push the barge.

INTERCARGO INTERnational association of dry CARGO ship owners.

INTERCOASTAL Domestic shipping routes serving more than one country from coast to coast.

INTERLOCUTARY ORDER, JUDGMENT One made or given during the progress of an action but which does not finally dispose of the rights of the parties.

INTERMODALISM The concept of transportation as a door-to-door service rather than port-to-port. Thus, efficiency is enhanced by having a single carrier coordinating the movement and documentation among different modes of transportation.

INTERNATIONAL LOAD LINE CERTIFICATE A certificate which gives details of a ship's freeboards and states that the ship has been surveyed and the appropriate load lines marked on her sides. This certificate is issued by a classification society or the Coast Guard.

INTERNATIONAL OIL POLLUTION COMPENSATION FUND An inter-governmental agency designed to pay compensation for oil pollution damage, exceeding the ship owner's liability. It was created by an IMO Convention in 1971 and started its operations in October 1978. Contributions come mainly from the oil companies of member states.

INTERNATIONAL TONNAGE CERTIFICATE A certificate issued to a ship owner by a government department in the case of a ship when gross and net tonnages have been determined in accordance with the International Convention of Tonnage Measurement of Ships. The certificate states the gross and net tonnages together with details of the spaces attributed to each.

INTERNATIONAL WATERWAYS Consist of international straits, inland and inter-ocean canals and rivers where they separate the territories of two or more nations. Provided no treaty is enforced, both merchant ships and warships have the right of free and unrestricted navigation through these waterways.

INTERTANKO An association of independent tanker owners whose aims are to represent the views of its members internationally.

INTRACOASTAL Domestic shipping routes along a single coast.

IOPP International Oil Pollution Certificate.

IOR Indian Ocean Region (INMARSAT).

IPSO FACTO (Latin) By the fact itself.

IRO In Respect Of.

ISF International Shipping Federation Ltd.

ISINGLASS A jelly obtained from the air bladder of various fish.

ISM CODE International Safety Management Code 1994. IMO regulation aimed at improving the management of vessels regarding their safety and to lessen the risk of pollution. Unfortunately the aim of the regulation has been largely diverted from its initial purpose to become a clerical business opportunity of its own.

ITF International Transport Workers Federation (Trade Unions).

ITINERARY Route/schedule.

ITU International Telecommunications Union.

ITZ Inshore Traffic Zone. Navigational lane which

lies between a TSS and the coast. May only be used by ships calling at a port or place inside the zone.
IWL Institute Warranty Limits.

J

J for JULIET   Morse = (. - - -)
Flag = horizontally divided in three with white in the middle and blue above and below. When hoisted singly from a ship it means 'I am going to send a semaphore signal.'

J2B Radio transmission designator. Telegraphy (automatic reception of), single-sideband (suppressed carrier) with a single channel containing quantified or digital information with the use of a modulating sub-carrier (ALRS).

J2DEN Radio transmission designator. Single-sideband suppressed carrier with a single channel containing quantified or digital information with the use of a modulating sub-carrier. Data transmission with a multi-condition code in which each condition represents a signal element (of one or more bits) and no multi-plexing (ALRS).

J3E Radio transmission designator. Telephony using amplitude modulation; single-sideband, suppressed carrier (ALRS).

JACK IN THE BASKET A short wooden cap or basket on the top of a pole to mark a sandbank or hidden danger.

JACK-UP RIG A deck with legs that can be jacked up or down. During operations, the legs rest on the sea bed. When the rig is moved the legs are retracted, leaving the rig floating. A jack-up rig has normally no propulsion machinery of its own.

JACOB'S LADDER Rope ladder with wooden round rungs light enough to be easily portable. It cannot be used as pilot ladder but is regularly used by the crew to check the draft or reach work staging.

JCC Joint Cargo Committee.

JCRA Joint Common Risk Agreement.

JERKED BEEF (Jerky) Beef dried in the sun.

JETSAM Part of a ship that has been thrown overboard. Jetsam went to the lord of the manor on whose land it washed up.

JETTISON The voluntary act of throwing goods overboard.

JETTY The projecting part of a wharf; a pier on which to land goods and passengers.

JHC Joint Hull Committee.

JHIU Japanese Hull Insurance Union.

JHU Joint Hull Understanding.

JIB Top part of a crane that can pivot and stretch out to pick up cargo for unloading ships.

JONES ACT Merchant Marine Act of 1920, Section 27, requiring that all US domestic waterborne trade be carried by US-flag, US-built and US-manned vessels.

JUMBOIZING Conversion of a ship to increase cargo-carrying capacity by dividing and adding a new section.

JURY-MAST A temporary mast erected in a vessel in the place of one which has been carried away in a gale etc.

JUTE A fibre used in making coarse canvas or gunny. Grown in India, Pakistan, Bangladesh.

JUTE ROVE Waste, made in spinning yarn; can be called spinning waste, ie dead ends of spoiled ends of yarn from the looms.

K

K for KILOGRAM   Morse = (– . –)
Flag = vertically divided with yellow at the hoist, blue at the fly. When hoisted singly from a ship it means 'Stop your vessel immediately'.

KAOLIN China clay. A clay derived from the decomposition of feldspar or granite. Used in the manufacture of porcelain, paper, medicine etc. Stows at about 35m³ per ton and is therefore heavier than coal.

KAPOK Cotton down enveloping seeds of the silk cotton tree. Used for stuffing chairs, pillows etc. Oil resembling cotton seed oil is obtained from kapok seed.

KEEL The lowest longitudinal part along the centre

line of a vessel, on which the framework of the whole is built up.

KEELAGE Dues paid by a ship making use of certain British ports.

KELP Large kinds of seaweed; calcinated ashes of seaweed, contains carbonate of soda, iodine etc.

KEROSENE The most important form of illuminating agent derived from petroleum. Also fuel for airplanes.

KILDERKIN A beer measure of 18 gallons.

KILOMETRE, km 1000 metres, 0.621371733 statute mile, 0.539612294 nautical mile, 1093.61425 yards.

KNOT Unit of speed in navigation. Nautical mile (6080 feet or 1852 metres) is equal to one minute of bow of the circumference of the globe.

L

L for LIMA   Morse = (. – . .)

Flag = two yellow and two black squares. When hoisted singly from a ship it means 'Stop, I have something important to communicate.'

LAC, SHELLAC A gum resin produced by an insect. Used in dyes, varnishes.

LADEN DRAUGHT Depth of water to which a ship is immersed when fully loaded.

LAFTA Latin American Free Trade Association.

LAGAN Goods jettisoned and sunk but attached to a buoy or floating object so that they may be found and recovered.

LAID UP A vessel is laid up when moored for want of employment.

LAID-UP TONNAGE Ship not in active service; a ship which is out of commission, awaiting better markets.

LAKER Type of ship which trades only in the Great Lakes of North America. Usually carries grain or ore cargoes.

LANDBRIDGE A transport system whereby cargo is hauled by rail over a long distance on land linking ports or specific destinations.

LANDLORD PORT Institutional structure whereby the port authority or other relevant public agency retains ownership of the land, as well as responsibility for maintaining approach channels and navigation aids; under this model, the port authority does not engage in any operational activities.

LANOLIN Sheep's wool grease, a by-product of the wool combing industry.

LARGET A length of iron cut from a bar and of proper size to roll into a sheet.

LASA Latin American Shipowners' Association.

LASH Lighter Aboard SHip. A barge carrier designed to act as a shuttle between ports, taking on and discharging barges. It is, in fact, a specialized container ship carrying very large floating containers or 'lighters'. The ship carries its own massive crane, which loads and discharges the containers over the stern. The lighters each have a capacity of 400 tons and are stowed in the holds and on deck. While the ship is at sea with one set of lighters, further sets can be made ready. Loading and discharge are rapid at about 15 minutes per lighter, no port or dock facilities are needed and the lighters can be grouped for pushing by towboats along inland waterways.

LAT Latitude. Distance directly north or south of the equator measured in degrees of the meridian.

LATEX The milky juice or sap of plants, mostly from the rubber tree.

LAY/CAN Lay days/cancelling. Range of dates within which the hire contract must start.

LAY DAYS, LAY TIME Time allowed by the ship owner to the voyage charterer or bill of lading holder in which to load and/or discharge the cargo. It is expressed as a number of days or hours or as a number of tons per day. Sundays and legal holidays do not count unless the term 'running days' has been inserted.

LAY-UP Temporary cessation of trading of a ship by a ship owner during a period when there is a surplus of ships in relation to the level of available cargoes. This surplus, known as over-tonnaging, has the effect of depressing freight rates to the extent that some ship owners no long find it economical to trade their ships, preferring to lay them up until there is a reversal in the trend.

LBP Length Between Perpendiculars. Length of the ship measured between two vertical lines corresponding more or less to the location where the loaded ship crosses the water line. Aft it positioned in relation to the rudder shaft. Th draughts marks are preferably placed in relation to these perpendiculars. This is the length used for most calculations. The frames are usually numbered from the aft perpendiculars.

L/C Letter of Credit.

LC50, Lethal Concentration 50 A concentration of a substance that produces death in 50% of a population of experimental animals after exposure for a period of time which is usually specified (eg '96 hour LC50'). This term is used when the substance exists in the organism's ambient environment at the specified concentration (for example, fish in water in which the substance is present at the specified concentration).

LD50, Lethal Dose 50 A dose of a substance that produces death in 50% of a population of experimental animals. It is usually expressed as milligrams per kilogram (mg/kg) of body weight. This term is used when the exposure pathway is by absorption of the specified dose.

L/D Load/Discharge. Brokers term: average load/discharge rate per day, in tons (L/D 6000/3000). Usually followed by more details about the method of counting the days.

LEAKAGE In a marine insurance policy means any loss of weight of the bulk during the course of the voyage.

LEASE A contract of letting lands, property or premises for a stipulated period to a person or company for a certain rent or other compensation.

LEASE-DEVELOP-OPERATE, LDO A form of concession wherein, under a long term lease, a private company upgrades and expands an existing facility and manages its cash flows. The public authority holds title to the facility throughout the concession period and receives lease payments on the assets.

LECCO Let go (mooring lines).

LEE-SHORE A vessel is said to be on a lee-shore when she is near it with the wind blowing right onto it.

LESSEE A person to whom a lease is granted.

LESSOR Person who grants a lease.

LESS THAN CONTAINER LOAD, LCL A consignment of cargo which is insufficient to fill a shipping container. It is grouped with other consignments for the same destination in a container at a container freight station.

LEVEL-LUFFING CRANE Crane built in such a

way that when the jib is topping, the lifted load remains level at the same hoisted height.

LHAR London, Hull, Antwerp, Rotterdam.

LIBA Lloyd's Insurance Brokers Association.

LIBC Lloyd's Insurance Brokers Committee.

LIBELLING a vessel. American term for 'arresting' a vessel.

LIEN Right to retain property until a creditor detaining it is satisfied. Goods carried by sea are subject to a lien for freight.

LIEUTENANT Deck Officer's rank below Captain. There is a First, Second, Third and Fourth Lieutenant. In the English navy the pronunciation is *leftenant*. On sailing ships the Fourth Lieutenant also served as 'doctor' and was therefore called 'Mister', not Lieutenant.

LIFEBOAT A specially constructed double ended boat that can withstand heavy, rough seas and used on board ship to be launched in case of emergency.

LIFEBOAT DRILL The Master of every vessel is bound by international law to make the Officers, crew and passengers adequately acquainted with the procedures of lowering and the use of lifeboats in case of emergency.

LIGHT DISPLACEMENT TONNAGE The weight of a ship's hull, machinery, equipment and spares. This is often the basis on which ships are paid for when purchased for scrapping.

LIGHT DUES Passing tolls levied on ships navigating certain waters towards the maintenance of a lighthouse etc.

LIGHTER General name for a broad, flat-bottomed boat used in transporting cargo between a vessel and the shore. The distinction between a lighter and a barge is more in the manner of use than in equipment. The term 'lighter' refers to a short haul, generally in connection with loading and unloading operations of vessels in harbour, while the term 'barge' is more often used when the cargo is being carried to its destination over a long distance.

LIGHTER ABOARD SHIP An ocean ship which carries barges. These barges are loaded with cargo, often at a variety of locations, towed to the ocean ship, sometimes referred to as the mother ship, and lifted or, in some cases, floated on board. After the ocean crossing, the barges are off-loaded and towed to their various destinations. The ocean ship then receives a further set of barges which have been assembled in readiness. This concept was designed to eliminate the need for specialized port equipment and to avoid trans-shipment with its consequent extra cost.

LIGHTERAGE The price paid for loading or unloading ships by lighters or barges.

LIGHTERING Conveying cargo with another vessel known as a lighter from ship to shore, or vice versa, also for making the ship lighter in order to reach lower draft ports for final discharge.

LIGHT SHIP A vessel with no cargo or merely in ballast.

LIMBERS The gutters on either side of the keel of a vessel or, where double bottom is fitted, at the side of the tanks, next to the margin plates.

LIMITATIONS (Statute of) If for six years no acknowledgement of a simple contract debt (as on an account or on a bill of exchange) has been made, the debtor may avoid payment of it by pleading this statute.

LIMITED RECOURSE FINANCING Project financing in which sponsors or governments agree to provide contingent financial support to give lenders extra comfort; typically provided during the construction and start-up period of a project, which is generally the riskiest time in the life of an infrastructure project.

LINE HAUL Movement of freight over the tracks of a transportation line from one city to another.

LINER A cargo-carrying ship which is operated between scheduled, advertized ports of loading and discharge on a regular basis.

LINER SERVICE Vessels operating on fixed itineraries or regular schedules and established rates available to all shippers. The freight rates which are charged are based on the shipping company's tariff or, if the company is a member of a liner conference, the tariff of that conference.

LINSEED Seed of the flax plant, exported in bags. Linseed oil is expressed from this seed and the residue is used in oilcake for fodder.

LIST Inclination of a ship to one side; when leaning over to one side of the perpendicular.

LLOYD'S An incorporated society of marine and non-marine underwriters at Lloyd's Building, Lime Street, London EC3.

LLOYD'S LIST Established in 1734. Publication collecting and disseminating shipping intelligence.

LLOYD'S REGISTER OF SHIPPING British classification society, 71 Fenchurch Street, London EC3, which formulates rules for the construction of vessels and assigns classes to them when the rules haven't been complied with. Surveyors supervize the construction and upkeep of vessels.

LLOYD'S SHIPPING INDEX Alphabetical list of names of ocean-going vessels of all nationalities, voyage details and latest reported positions. Published daily from Monday to Friday.

LMC Lloyd's Machinery Certificate.

LMT Local Mean Time.

LNG Liquefied Natural Gas.

LNG CARRIER Liquefied natural gas carrier, perhaps the most sophisticated of all commercial ships. The cargo tanks are made of a special alloy and are heavily insulated to carry natural gas in its liquid state at a temperature of -285°F. Transport on board is at around −161°C whereby 1cbm of LNG represents 6000cbm of gas.

LOA Length Over All. Length measured between the two extremities of the vessel.

LOADED LEG Part of a ship's voyage during which it is carrying cargo.

LOAD FACTOR Percentage of cargo or passengers carried eg 4000 tons carried on a vessel of 10,000 tons capacity has a load factor of 40%.

LOAD LINE The line on a vessel indicating the maximum depth to which that vessel may sink when loaded with cargo. Also known as marks, derived from the 'Plimsoll mark'.

LOF Lloyd's Open Form.

LOI Letter Of Indemnity. In the past it was a letter allowing a Clean Bill of Lading to be signed even if the goods shipped were known to have a default or shortage, the Letter offering a guarantee that it was recognized by the shipper. Lately it is also a Letter presented by the receiver of the cargo for the delivery of the cargo without presenting an original Bill of Lading. This practice should only be valid if the C/P mentions this possibility.

LO-LO, LIFT ON-LIFT OFF Type of vessel that allows cargo to be loaded or unloaded by either ship or shore cranes.

LONG Longitude. Distance east or west on the Earth's surface of a given meridian and is reckoned in degrees which vary in length according to the latitude where the longitude is reckoned. Longitude can also be measured in time as well as degrees, the

Earth turning through an angle of 1 degree (or 60 minutes) of longitude in 4 minutes of time. The time at a place situated east of the meridian of Greenwich is 'fast on Greenwich', a place west is 'slow on Greenwich'.

LONGSHOREMAN Individual employed locally in a port to load and unload ships (also: docker or dockworker).

LONG TON 2240 pounds or 1016.05 kilograms. *See LT.*

LOOKOUT A member of the crew stationed on the forecastle or on the bridge, whose duty it is to watch for any dangerous objects or for any other vessels in the vicinity.

LOOP A sequence of ports at each end of the voyage.

LORAN System of finding the position of the ship on the map by radio signals, mainly used in the past along the US coast.

LPG Liquefied Petroleum Gas. Gases produced by the treatment of crude oil, usually carried in semi-pressurized (5/7 bars) and fully pressurized (18 bars) semi or fully refrigerated LPG tankers.

LPP Length between perpendiculars. On the waterline a perpendicular line is drawn at the front and rear of the vessel, the distance between these perpendiculars being the LPP.

LR Lloyd's Register. British Classification Society.

LRQA Lloyd's Register Quality Assurance.

LSA Liner Shipping Agreement.

LSF Lloyd's Standard Form of Salvage Agreement, 'no cure, no pay'. Also called 'Open form'.

LSS Loading Sequence Sheet.

LSSD Lloyd's Syndicates Survey Department.

LST Local Standard Time.

LT Long Ton. Mostly used in the USA. Its value is 1.01605 metric tons or 1016.05 kilograms.

LTA Long Term Agreement.

LTS Lay Time Saved.

LUFFING, TOPPING Movement of the crane whereby the jib is brought closer to the driver's cabin.

LUMBER American term for timber sawn or split for use.

LUMPSUM FREIGHT Money paid to shipper for charter of a ship (or portion) up to stated limit irrespective of quantity of cargo.

LW Low Water.

LWOST Low Water Ordinary Spring Tide.

M

Flag = Diagonal white cross on blue background. When hoisted singly from a ship it means 'I have a doctor on board'.

MAC VALUE Maximum Acceptable Concentration value. The MAC value is the upper limit of concentration of a substance in air, which according to present knowledge, does not provoke illness in the large majority of healthy persons exposed to it, even if the exposure is for relatively long periods of 8 hours per day and 40 hours per week. The substance can be in the form of a gas, a vapour or a powder (mg/m3).

MAGAZINE A warehouse; a place for storing explosives, ashore or afloat.

MAIN DECK The main continuous deck of a ship running from fore to aft; the principal deck; the deck from which the freeboard is determined.

MAIZE The general name for seeds of Indian corn. 1 ton is estimated to measure 50 cubic feet in bulk and 10% more in bags.

MALACCA-MAX Maximum size ships (container ships and bulkers) that can cross the Malacca Strait. The Malacca-max reference is currently the maximum size for container ships.

MANAGEMENT CONTRACT Arrangement whereby the operation and management of a facility is contracted by the port authority to a specialized operator for a specified period and under specified conditions relating to performance criteria, economic incentives, maintenance and infrastructure commitments etc. The public authority retains ownership of the facility and the commercial risk associated with its operation.

MANGANESE A metal like iron, used for toughening and hardening steel.

MANIFEST A document containing a full list of the ship's cargo, extracted from the bills of lading, setting out the distinguishing marks and numbers, also the weight and description of each package of goods, the shipper's and consignee's name etc, signed by the Master.

MANNING SCALES The minimum number of Officers and crew members that can be engaged on a ship to be considered as sufficient hands with practical ability to meet every possible eventuality at sea.

MARINE INSURANCE A contract of marine insurance is a contract whereby the insurer undertakes to indemnify the assured in the manner and to the extent thereby agreed, against marine loss or incident to the marine adventure. A marine insurance policy secures an indemnity against accidents which may happen, not against events which must happen.

MARITIME ADMINISTRATION, MARAD Oversees subsidy programmes to the United States Merchant Marine Assigned routes to subsidized liners.

MARITIME LIEN A claim which attaches to the ship, freight or cargo.

MARITIME SUBSIDY BOARD, MSB A branch within the Maritime Administration which deals with Operating Differential Subsidy and Construction Differential Subsidy.

MARPOL 73/78 The International Convention for the Prevention of Pollution from Ships, 1973, as modified by the Protocol of 1978. This is a set of regulation aimed at preventing pollution by oil, chemicals, noxious substances, garbage and sewage.

MARS Marine Accident Reporting Scheme. Created by the Nautical Institute, *NI*, the reports are anonymous and do not provide any name of persons, ships or companies. They are published monthly in the NI publication *Seaways*.

MASTER'S PROTEST See *Protest*.

MASTHEAD LIGHT A white light positioned over the fore and aft centre line of the vessel and covering from straight ahead to two points abaft the beam.

MATE'S RECEIPT Document presented to the Chief Mate for his signature as recognition for having received the cargo on board. This document is the basis from which the Bill of Lading is than prepared.

MAYDAY Signal of distress by radio telephony. Equivalent to SOS in Morse Code.

M/D Months after Date.

MEPC Maritime Environment Protection Committee. IMO branch dealing, among other issues, with the construction of tankers. The number of the meeting is often added to the acronym so that in Autumn 2000 the meeting was MEPC46.

METHANE CH$_4$ Natural gas carried in great quantities by LNG tankers at boiling temperature (-161°C).

METRIC TONNE 2204.6223lbs.

MFN Most Favoured Nation.

MH Main Hatch.

MHWS Mean High Water Spring tide.

MIB Marine Index Bureau.

MICA A transparent mineral in flakes.

MICROBRIDGE A system of through rates and services offered by a carrier for cargo shipments from any inland US location to a port, by sea to a foreign port and finally overland to foreign inland destination.

MILLET A common name for several species of small seed corn.

MILLIBAR, mb Unit of atmospheric pressure: 1 millibar = 0.750076 millimetre of mercury = 0.0295306 inch of mercury.

MILLISIEVERT, mSv The measure of potential biological damage to specific body organs or tissues caused by exposure to and subsequent absorption of radiation is expressed in a unit of measure known as a rem. One rem of any type of radiation has the same total damaging effect. Because a rem represents a fairly large dose equivalent, dose equivalents are expressed as fractions of a rem, millirem (mrem), which is 1/1000 of a rem. In the international system of units, 1 sievert (Sv) equals 100 rem; 1 millisievert (mSv) equals 100 mrem. Specific types of dose equivalents are defined as follows:

- Committed dose equivalent: the total dose equivalent to an organ during the 50 year period following intake.

- Effective dose equivalent (EDE): the weighted sum of dose equivalents to a specified list of organs. The organs and weighting factors are selected on the basis of risk to the entire body. EDE is the unit used in the Annual Site Environmental Report committed effective dose equivalent: the total effective dose to specified organs in the human body during the 50 year period following intake.

- Collective effective dose equivalent: the sum of effective dose equivalents of all members of a given population.

MIN Minimum.

MINI LAND BRIDGE The process of taking inland cargo bound for export to the coast by rail and loading it directly onto the ship.

MINUTE *1* Sixtieth part of an hour. *2* Sixtieth part of a degree. Also brief summary of proceedings of a meeting.

MIRAID Maritime Institute for Research and Industrial Development.

MISSING VESSEL An overdue vessel considered lost and posted in the records at Lloyd's as 'missing'.

MIXED SHIPMENT A shipment consisting of more than one commodity, articles described under more than one class or commodity rate item in a tariff.

MMSI Maritime Mobile Selective-call Identity code. New compulsory code to identify vessels with the GMDSS/DSC system.

MOA Memorandum Of Agreement. Sometimes also MOU (Understanding).

MOBILE CRANE General purpose crane capable of being moved from one part of a port to another.

MODU Mobile Offshore Drilling Unit.

MOH Medical Officer of Health.

MOLASSES The syrup that drains from raw sugar or from sugar during the process of refining. In English the latter is also called 'treacle'.

MOLE A long pier of massive masonry; a breakwater forming an artificial harbour.

MOLOO More Or Less in Owner's Option. Chartering term: range of weights of the goods to be shipped. Often expressed in percentage: MOLOO 50,000; 10% = 45,000 to 55,000 tons.

MOOR To attach a ship to the shore by ropes or wires.

MOORING LINE A cable or line to tie up a ship.

MORTGAGE Loan issued against some security.

MOTHER-OF-PEARL Smooth shining forming of inner layer of some shells.

MPH Miles Per Hour.

MS Machinery Survey.

M/S Months after Sight.

MSB Maritime Subsidy Board.

MSC Marine Safety Committee (IMO).

MSCN Maritime Simulation Centre Netherlands. Located at Wageningen, it was also known under its place name.

MSD *1* Marine Sanitation Device. Any equipment installed on board a vessel to receive, retain, treat, or discharge sewage and any process to treat such sewage.

2 Material Safety Data sheets. Detailed information about the dangerous products carried.

MT Mean Time. Also Motor Tanker.

M/T Metric Tons (1000kg or 2205lbs).

MTC Maritime Transport Committee, OECD.

MTL Mean Tidal Level.

MULTIPURPOSE SHIP Any ship capable of carrying different types of cargo which require different methods of handling. There are several types of ships falling into this category, for example ships which can carry roll on/roll off cargo together with containers.

MUST Grape juice.

N for NOVEMBER   Morse = (– .)

Flag = four horizontal rows of alternating blue and white squares. When hoisted singly from a ship it means 'No – Negative.'

NAABSA Not Always Afloat But Safe Aground.

NATIONAL CARGO BUREAU A private organization with representatives throughout the main harbours in the US. It is empowered to inspect cargoes of a hazardous nature and issue certificates which are automatically approved by the Coast Guard.

NATIONAL FLAG The flag carried by a ship to show her nationality.

NATURAL RESOURCES (US/OPA 90) Includes land, fish, wildlife, biota, air, water, groundwater, drinking water supplies and other such resources belonging to, managed by, held in trust by, appertaining to, or otherwise controlled by the United States (including the resources of the exclusive economic zone), any State, local government, Indian tribe or any foreign government. The ship's staff should be aware of them.

NAUTICAL MILE 6080ft, 1853.1824m.

NCNP No Cure, No Pay. Salvage contract term. *See also LOF.*

NEAP TIDES *See Tides.*

NEATSFOOT OIL Oil obtained from the feet of cattle. Used for softening and preserving leather.

NEGLIGENCE Absence of care according to the circumstances.

NEO-BULK Shipments consisting entirely of

uniformly packaged units of a single commodity such as cars, timber in bundles, drums on pallets, big bags or scrap metal.

NET Not subject to deduction.

NET CAPACITY The number of tons of cargo which a vessel can carry when loaded in salt water to her summer freeboard marks. Also called cargo carrying capacity, cargo deadweight, useful deadweight.

NET FORM CHARTER *See Bare boat charter.*

NET TERMS Free of charterer's commission.

NET TONNAGE Equals gross tonnage minus deductions for space occupied by crew accommodation, machinery, navigation equipment and bunkers. It represents space available for cargo (and passengers). Canal tolls are based on net (registered) tonnage. Reckoned in units of 100 cubic feet (2.8317 cubic metres).

NH3 *See Ammonia.*

NHP Nominal Horse Power.

NI Nautical Institute. Organization founded in 1971, located in London, which promotes high professional standards among Deck Officers. Email sec@nautinst.org website www.nautinst.org.

NICKEL Hard, silvery, white, lustrous, malleable, ductile metal associated with cobalt.

NITRATE Nitrate of soda from Chile, used as fertilizer. Now also produced chemically.

NK Nippon Kaiji kyokai. Japanese Classification Society.

NKORL No Known Or Reported Loss.

NOC Notice Of Cancellation.

NOMINEE One who is nominated by another.

NON BUSINESS DAYS Sunday, Good Friday, Christmas Day, a bank holiday under Bank Holidays Act 1871 or acts amending it and a day appointed by royal proclamation as a public fast or thanksgiving day. Any other day is a business day in Britain.

NON-CONFERENCE LINE A shipping line which operates on a route served by a liner conference but which is not a member of that conference, also called 'outsider'.

NONCONTIGUOUS Domestic shipping routes serving Alaska and non-continental US states and territories.

NOR Notice Of Readiness.

NORSKE VERITAS, DET Norwegian classification society.

NORTHERN RANGE US Atlantic ports: Norfolk,

Newport News, Baltimore, Philadelphia, New York, Boston and Portland (Great Lakes).

NR No Risk until confirmed. Net Register.

NRAD No Risk After Discharge.

NRDA Natural Resources Damage Assessment (USA).

NRT Net Registered Tons. This tonnage is frequently shown on ship registration papers. It represents the volumetric area available for cargo at 100 cubic feet = 1 ton. It is often used by port and canal authorities as a basis for charges.

NSPF Not Specially Provided For.

NTSB National Transportation Safety Board (US). US agency investigating accidents in the transport industries. Most likely the best in the world.

NUN BUOY Buoy tapering at each end.

NVOCC Non-Vessel-Operating Common Carrier. A ship's agent, conducts business for the ship but does not operate the vessel. Acts as consolidator in ocean trade who buys space from a carrier. He issues bills of lading, publishes tariffs and otherwise conducts himself as an ocean common carrier except that he does not provide the actual ocean or inter-modal service.

O for OSCAR   Morse = (– – –)

Flag = halved diagonally in red and yellow. When hoisted singly from a ship it means 'Man overboard'.

OA Over All.

O/A On Account of.

OAKUM Loose fibre got by picking old rope to pieces and used especially for caulking.

OBO Ore/Bulk/Oil vessel.

OBO SHIP A multipurpose ship that can carry ore, heavy dry bulk goods and oil. Although more expensive to build, it is ultimately more economical because it can make return journeys with cargo rather than empty as single-purpose ships often must.

OC *1* Open Charter.
2 Overcharge.

OCC Operations Control Centre (INMARSAT).

OCEAN WAYBILL A document, issued by a

shipping line to a shipper, which serves as a receipt for the goods and evidence of the contract carriage.

OCIMF Oil Companies International Maritime Forum.

ODS Operating Differential Subsidy. A direct subsidy paid to US-flag operators to offset the high operating cost of US-flag ships when compared with foreign-flag counterparts.

OECD Organization for Economic Cooperation and Development. The Maritime Transport Committee is part of this organization.

OFF-HIRE CLAUSE In a time charter, the owner is entitled to a limited time for his vessel to be off hire until such time as the vessel may be repaired or dry-docked.

OFFICER Any of the licensed members of the ship's complement.

OFFING Implies to seaward, beyond anchoring ground. To keep a good offing is to keep well off the land while under sail.

OFF-LOAD Discharging of cargo from a ship.

OFFSHORE SERVICE VESSELS Special vessels employed in servicing oil platforms that are exploring or continuously producing sub-sea oil and gas.

OILER An unlicensed member of the engine room staff who oils and greases bearings and moving parts of the main engine and auxiliaries. Most of this work is now done automatically and the oiler merely insures it operates correctly.

OIL RECORD BOOK A book or log kept by the master of an oil tanker wherein every loading, discharge or escape of oil is recorded.

OIL TANKER A ship designed for the carriage of oil in bulk, her cargo space consisting of several or many tanks. Tankers load their cargo by gravity from the shore and discharge using their own pumps.

OLEAGINOUS Containing oil.

OLEIFEROUS Oil producing.

ON-CARRIER Person or company who contracts to transport cargo from the port of discharge of a sea-going ship to another destination by different means of transport, such as truck, train or barge.

OO Owner's Option.

OP Open or floating Policy. *See Open policy.*

OPA 90 Oil Pollution Act 1990 (US Public law 101-380 18 August 1990). US legislation dealing with oil pollution and drafted after the grounding of the

Exxon Valdez. The main points are the fitting of a double hull on tankers and *unlimited responsibility* of the ship owner if pollution is not reported.

OPEC Organization of Petroleum Exporting Countries.

OPEN CHARTER Vessel can be fixed for any port with any cargo.

OPEN POLICY One in which a maximum amount is stated and the goods insured are allowed to be shipped in varying amounts in one or more vessels up to the maximum sum but within the general terms of the policy. In an open policy, where the value shipped does not equal the value insured, the difference is termed 'over insurance' and the proportionate amount of the premium returnable to the insurer is called 'return for short interest'.

OPEN RATES Pricing systems that are flexible and not subject to conference approval. Usually applied to products in which tramps are substituted for liners.

OPEN REGISTRY A term used in place of 'flag of convenience' or 'flag of necessity' to denote registry in a country which offers favourable tax, regulatory and other incentives to ship owners from other nations.

OPEN SHIP Dry cargo vessel whereby the holds are constructed as neat squares so that cargo can be deposited without any lateral movement.

OPIUM The resinous gum or juice of the white poppy.

OPRC Oil pollution Preparedness, Response and Cooperation.

OPTION Purchased right to call for or make delivery within specified time of stocks etc at a specified price.

OPTIONAL CARGO Cargo that is destined for one of the ship's discharge ports, the exact one not being known when the goods are loaded.

OR Owner's Risk.

ORDINARY LOSS The usual expected loss sustained by liquids and various kinds of merchandise during a voyage under normal circumstances.

ORE-BULK-OIL CARRIER A large multi-purpose ship designed to carry cargoes whether of ore or other bulk commodities or oil so as to reduce the time the ship would be in ballast if restricted to one type of commodity. This type of ship is sometimes called a bulk-oil carrier.

ORE CARRIER A large ship designed to be used for the carriage of ore. Because of the high density of ore, ore carriers have a relatively high double bottom, bringing the centre of gravity higher up to prevent heavy and short period rolling at sea.

ORE-OIL CARRIER A ship designed to carry either ore or oil in bulk.

ORDINARY SEAMAN A deck crew member who is subordinate to the Able Bodied Seamen.

ORIENT (French) East: referring to China, Japan, Philippines

OSP One Safe Port.

OSSEIN Dry acid treated bones, used in gelatine manufacture.

OST Ordinary Spring Tides.

OT On Truck.

OUTSIDER A ship operator not part of a conference.

OVERCARRIAGE The carriage of cargo beyond the port for which it was intended.

OVERHEAD CHARGES Salaries, expenses and establishment charges.

OVERTONNAGING A situation where there are too many ships generally or in a particular trade for the level of available cargoes.

OVOIDS Patent fuel, similar in substance to the ordinary domestic coal block. Manufactured in moulds and approximately 3 inches in length and about 5 inches in circumference. When this cargo is loaded it is advizable to provide shifting boards.

OWNER, SHIP OWNER The formal owner of a ship although, more and more, he does not invest much money himself but gets a loan from financial institutions who trust his management. On some small ships the owner can be the Captain. This was regularly the case in Greece but recently the Dutch reverted to this system on some coasters as this is the best way to have a Master highly motivated to defend the interests of the ship.

OXIDIZING AGENT IMDG CODE 5.1 A chemical or substance that brings about an oxidation reaction. The agent may:

(1) provide the oxygen to the substance being oxidized (in which case the agent has to be oxygen or contain oxygen), or

(2) receive electrons being transferred from the substance undergoing oxidation. (Chlorine is a good oxidizing agent for electron-transfer purposes, even though it contains no oxygen).

P

P for PAPA Morse = (. – – .)

Flag = white square on a blue background. Referred to as 'Blue Peter'. When hoisted singly from a ship it means 'The ship is going to sail'.

PA Particular Average.

PACKAGE The term includes crate, sack, hamper, bundle or other article or means wherein or whereby a commodity is conveyed.

PACSCAT Partial Air Cushion Support Catamaran.

PADRONE (Italian) A Master who by Italian law is not allowed to command a vessel outside the Mediterranean.

PALLET A flat tray, generally made of wood but occasionally of steel, on which goods in boxes, cartons or bags can be stacked. Its purpose is to facilitate the movement of such goods, mainly by the use of forklift trucks.

PANAMA CANAL TONNAGE Here vessels require a special tonnage certificate as the method of computing the Gross Tonnage differs in a few details from the ordinary system.

PANAMAX A vessel designed to fit the passage of the locks in the Panama Canal (900 x 100 feet).

P&I CLUB Protection and Indemnity Club.

PARAFFIN A colourless, tasteless, odorousless, crystalline, fatty substance, solid at ordinary temperatures, obtained by dry distillation from wood, coal, peat, petroleum, wax and other substances and also occurring native in coal and other bituminous strata. Used to make candles etc.

PARAFFIN OIL A clear oily liquid, obtained from petroleum after the more volatile portions have been removed by distillation. Used as an illuminant and a lubricant.

PARTICULAR AVERAGE Damage or loss to a vessel or cargo purely accidental in nature and not damage or expense voluntarily incurred for the benefit of all concerned. Any loss applying to particular interest and not affecting the rest.

PASSENGER SHIP A ship built especially for the carriage of passengers.

PATENT FUEL Cola blocks made of coal dust mixed with 7% to 9% of gas pitch as a binder and heated by superheated steam to bind the mixture together and then moulded under pressure. These blocks can be stored for years without any appreciable loss of heating powers. *See also Ovoids.*

PAX PASSENGERS Unit of measurement of people who pay to be on board. Theoretically, an organization settled by a group of owners to insure among other liabilities not covered by the Hull and Machinery insurances.

PCC Pure Car Carriers. Vessel type, able to carry several thousand cars.

PCS Pieces.

PCTC Pure Car/Truck Carriers. Vessel type.

PD Paid. Passed.

PDI Pre-Delivery Inspection. Value added service by inspecting shipped goods when they leave the sea carrier.

PDO Physical Damage Only.

PER Through; by means of; according to.

PER CONTAINER RATE Rates charged for the transport of containers.

PERILS OF THE SEA Something involving the fortuitous and unexpected.

PERMANENT DUNNAGE Strips of timber fixed to the frames of a ship to keep cargo from the sides of the ship in order to avoid damage and condensation.

PERMIT A licence to remove excisable goods.

PER SE (Latin) By itself or themselves; considered apart.

PERSONAL FLOTATION DEVICE Approved floats meant as life preservers and carried on board American ships.

PETIT-GRAIN An essential oil obtained from the fruit and leaves of bitter oranges.

PETROL Refined petroleum used in internal combustion engines.

PETROLEUM A mineral oil.

PIASSAVA The footstalks of a species of palm. Shipped in bundles and used for making brushes and street-sweeping machines. Exported from Brazil and West Africa.

PICKLING Jute cloth used for protecting and separating grain cargo in a vessel.

PIER Structure perpendicular to the shoreline to which a vessel is secured for the purpose of loading and unloading cargo.

PIGGY PACKER A mobile container-handling crane used to (un)load containers to/from railway wagons.

PIG IRON Oblong masses of iron. It is cast-iron of the first fusion and exists in various grades. Foundry pig used for iron castings. Gorge pig used for puddle wrought iron. Steel making pig used for making carbon steel varying in quality and character for different steel making processes.

PIG OF LEAD Weighs 154lbs.

PILFERAGE Stealing of small quantities of goods. Petty theft.

PILOT A person who is qualified to assist the Master of a ship to navigate when entering or leaving a port. Experienced local navigator who advises the Master about the peculiarities of the port and its approaches. Practically, the pilot himself directs the manœuvring of the vessel by giving steering orders to the helmsman and engine orders to the ship's Mate. On some difficult waterways (Manchester and Scheldt – Brussels canals) the pilot or an assistant steers the ship directly. The pilot is almost never responsible, except on the Panama Canal, where his fault involves the liability of the canal authorities. In practice, this is limited by the numerous letters of 'release of liability' if the ship has some handicaps such as a bad trim. When the liability of the canal is in any way involved, the serious delay caused by the investigation of any incident means that it is cheaper not to report minor damage to the ship.

PILOTAGE The act carried out by a pilot of assisting the Master of a ship in navigation when entering or leaving a port. Sometimes used to define the fee payable for the services of a pilot.

PILOTAGE DUES A fee payable by the owner or operator of a ship for the services of a pilot. This fee is normally based on the ship's tonnage.

PILOT HOUSE The enclosed space on the navigating bridge from which a ship is controlled when under way, also 'bridge' or 'wheelhouse'.

PIMENTO, ALLSPICE Dried herbs of a West Indian tree, the Eugenia pimento. Used as a spice and has a flavour between peppers and cloves.

PIMENTO OIL Aromatic oil obtained from the fruit of the Eugenia pimento.

PITCH A distillate of tar.

PL 361 Tariff Act of 1930. Imposes a 50% tariff on maintenance and repair work done on US-flag vessels in foreign shipyards. Also, US-flag vessels must either be built in the United States or have been a US-flag vessel for at least 3 years to be eligible to carry preference cargo.

PL 480 Agricultural Trade Development and Assistance Act of 1954.

PL 664 Mandates that 50% of government impelled cargoes be carried under US flag. Known as the 50/50 shipping law.

P/L Partial loss.

PLATFORM FLAT A shipping container without sides, ends or roof. Normally 20 or 40 feet long, used for awkwardly shaped cargo that cannot fit on or into any other type of container. Usually stowed on top of a pile of containers.

PLC Public Limited Company.

PLIMSOLL'S MARK The mark to indicate the limit to which a ship can be loaded. The mark is carved and painted on both sides of the ship at mid-length, showing the deepest draft at which the ship may be loaded. Imposed by Mr Samuel Plimsoll in Britain in 1876. Several levels are indicated: SW = Summer sea water draft, TW = Tropical sea water draft, W = Winter sea water draft, WNA = Winter North Atlantic, FW = Summer fresh water draft, TFW = Tropical fresh water draft.

PMA Pacific Maritime Association.

PMCC Pensky-Martens Closed Cup. One of several types of apparatus for determining flash points. The Pensky-Martens closed tester (ASTM D93-79) is used for liquids that have a viscosity of 45 SUS (Saybolt universal seconds) or more at 100°F (38°C), a flash point of 200°F (93.6°C) or higher, contain suspended solids or form surface films.

POLICY Document containing the contract of insurance.

POLLARD Bran sifted from flour; a finer grade of bran containing some flour; also flour or meal containing the finer bran.

POLYMERIZATION Linking of small molecules (monomers) to form larger molecules (polymers). The molecular weight and structure of a polymer is determined by reaction factors such as temperature and pressure and concentrations of reactants, monomer, catalyst or initiator and modifying agents. Polymerization may occur by addition reactions or by condensation as in the production of polyamides, polyesters and polysulphides. A real risk on a chemical tanker and when it happens the tank contains a solid block of plastic instead of a liquid.

PONTOON A flat-bottomed shallow draught vessel.

POOLING The sharing of cargo or the profit or loss from freight by member lines of a liner conference. Pooling arrangements do not exist in all conferences.

POONAC The cake left after expressing the oil from coconut pulp. Used for feeding animals, also as fertilizer.

POOP, POOP DECK Raised rear part of the vessel.

POR Pacific Ocean Region (INMARSAT).

PORT Formerly called 'Larboard'. The left side of a vessel looking towards the bow or forepart.

PORTABLE UNLOADER Type of ship unloader that is wheeled and capable of being moved around a port wherever needed. Typically used in ports where there is no dedicated terminal with its own fixed equipment.

PORTAGE-BILL Register or account of the names and claims for wages, allowances etc of the crew of a ship.

PORT DUES Charges levied against a ship owner or ship operator by a port authority for the use of a port.

PORT OF REFUGE Port, not on a ship's itinerary, where she calls owing to some unforeseen hazard at sea and where she may seek 'safe haven' or undergo repairs, refuel or rescue cargo.

PORT OF REGISTRY Place where a ship is registered with the authorities, thereby establishing its nationality.

PORT SIDE The left side of the vessel when facing forward. *See Starboard.*

PORT STATE CONTROL, PSC The organization in ports responsible for the control of seaworthiness of ships technically or as far as manning is concerned.

POSH Port Out, Starboard Home. The best and most expensive cabins on the former British steamers sailing to and from India. In the Mediterranean, the Red Sea and the Arabian Sea the sun was mainly on starboard side during the outbound trip and, of course, on the other side when the vessel was coming back. Now this acronym is used to designate somebody wealthy or 'upper-class'. Taking into account the poor performances of the air conditioning on many commercial ships it could still be useful to check from which side the sun will shine for a crossing.

POST After. Post date. To date a document in advance of the real date.

POSTED FOR INFORMATION Indicates that a notice has been issued by the Committee of Lloyd's asking for information concerning an overdue vessel and is a preliminary step to posting her as a 'missing vessel', which, in the event of no further news being received, usually follows seven days after the date of the notice.

POSTE RESTANTE Post office department where letters remain until called for.

POST MERIDIEM Pertaining to a period after noon, better known as PM.

POTASH Name applied to several compounds of potassium. Valuable as an artificial fertilizer.

POWER OF ATTORNEY Document which empowers one person to act for another.

PP, PPD Pre Paid. Prepaid, usually concerning the freight.

PP Picked Ports. Also 'per procurationem'.

PPI Policy Proof of Interest.

PPT Prompt.

PPT/ONW Prompt/(On Wharf). Broker's term: cargo is ready to be loaded.

PR-17 Public Resolution which requires that US Government financed cargoes (Exim bank) must be shipped 100% on US flag ships but that the requirement may be waived up to 50% in some cases.

PRATIQUE Licence or permission for a vessel to communicate freely with the shore after the production of a clean bill of health or after having performed quarantine (free pratique).

PREAMBLE Introduction to a charter party.

PRE-ENTRY Presentation to customs of export or import declarations prior to the clearance of goods.

PREMIUM Payment made for insurance. The difference in value above the original price or par of stock. Bonus.

PRIMAGE Percentage added to the freight; paid by the owners or freighters of the vessel.

PRIME COST Price of production, without regard to profit.

PRODUCT CARRIER A tanker which is generally below 70,000 deadweight tons and used to carry refined oil products from the refinery to the consumer, or chemicals. In many cases, different grades of oil or different chemical products can be handled simultaneously.

PRODUCTION UNIT Equipped to extract petroleum, eg oil production ship.

PROFORMA ACC Estimated account.

PROMPT Chartering. Vessel to start loading from 2 to 8 days but sometimes according to trade vessel's charter could not be cancelled under 14 days.

PROPANE C_3H_8 Petroleum gas carried on LPG tankers. Flash point = -105, boiling point = -3, auto-ignition = 460, all in degrees Celsius. Molecular weight = 44. Flammable range = 2 – 11pc.

PROPANE CARRIER A ship designed to carry propane in liquid form. The propane is carried in tanks within the holds; it remains in liquid form by means of pressure and refrigeration. Such ships are also suitable for the carriage of butane.

PRO RATA (Latin) Proportionately.

PRO TEMPORE (Latin) For the time being.

PROTEST A sworn statement by the Master, Officers and crew, or some of them, giving particulars of the voyage or any bad weather or accident encountered and of the course which, under any circumstances of emergency, the Master had taken. A protest is made before a notary public or Consul whenever possible.

PROTOCOL Original draft or diplomatic document especially of terms of treaty agreed in conference and signed by the parties.

PROVISO A conditional clause in any legal document on the observance of which its validity depends.

PROXY A deputy. Stamped power of attorney or authority to vote or act for another.

PRS Polish Register of Shipping. Classification societies. In 1997 it was rejected from the IACS group on a claim of low standards.

PSC Port State Control. Convention which allows the contracting states to inspect vessels calling at their ports and detain them if safety deficiencies are observed.

PSV Platform Supply Vessel. Carries supplies to drilling units or installations during field development or production.

PULPWOOD Short lengths of whitewood or spruce, 3 inches and upwards in diameter, used for grinding into pulp to make paper.

PULSE Edible seeds of leguminous plants like peas, beans and lentils.

PUMPMAN A rating who tends to the pumps of an oil tanker.

PURGING The introduction of inert gas content to a level already in the inert condition with the object of:
(1) Further reducing the existing oxygen content, and/or
(2) Reducing the existing hydrocarbon gas content to a level below which combustion cannot be supported if air is subsequently introduced into the tank.

PURSER A Ship's Officer who is in charge of accounts, especially on a passenger ship.

PV Pilot Vessel.

PYRINA Olive stone cakes.

PYRITES Sulphide of iron, sulphide of copper and iron, both used in the manufacture of sulphuric acid.

Flag = yellow. When hoisted singly from a ship it means 'Quarantine flag'. Hoisted on arrival, it means 'Nobody can go ashore or board until the Quarantine Officer has cleared the ship'.

QED (Latin) Quod Erat Demonstrandum, which was to be demonstrated or proven.

QUALIFIED MEMBER OF THE ENGINE DEPARTMENT (OMED) Unlicensed members of the engine department who attend to a fully automated engine room.

QUANTUM (Latin) Quantity or amount.

QUANTUM MERUIT (Latin) As much as deserved.

QUARANTINE Period of detention and isolation imposed upon vessels capable of carrying contagion.

QUARTER A grain measure of 8 bushels. Wheat, rye and maize weigh 480lbs; barley 400lbs; oats 320lbs.

QUARTERMASTER/HELMSMAN An Able Bodied Seaman entrusted with the steering of a vessel.

QUARTERS Accommodation.

QUASH To overthrow or annul.

QUAYAGE The charge for using a berth alongside a wharf.

QUAY WALL Construction alongside which ships

can moor. Made of concrete blocks, sheet piling or a combination of piles linked on top by a platform.

QUEBEC STANDARD A measure of timber consisting of 100 pieces, 12ft by 11in by 2.5in = 229.5 cu ft.

QUEBRACHO Tanning extract obtained from the wood of a South American tree.

QUEEN'S WAREHOUSE Where goods seized by customs are stored.

QUICKSILVER Commercial name for mercury. The heaviest of all fluids and has the appearance of melted silver.

QUID PRO QUO (Latin) One thing for another; an equivalent.

QUIRE OF PAPER 24 sheets, 20th part of a ream.

QUOD EST (Latin) Which is.

QUOD VIDE (Latin) Which see. (Also qv.)

QUORUM (Latin) A legal sufficient number of a committee to hold a meeting or to transact a business.

QUOTATION Current price of anything.

R

R for ROMEO   Morse = (. − .)

Flag = red background with yellow Greek cross. When hoisted singly from a ship it means 'The way is off my ship.'

R3E Telephony using amplitude modulation; single sideband; reduced carrier (ALRS).

RACKING Distorting of a ship's transverse shape through undue strain. This can now still happen with a large bulk carrier in bad weather. Some loading software can calculate the static racking due to uneven cargo distribution: torque.

RACON RAdar beaCONs. Radar signature of beacons and buoys for easy identification on the radar PPI. Most of them work on 3 and 10cm and if not they cannot be detected. Poor functioning also affects their performance, nevertheless, they offer an important aid to navigation.

RADIO OPERATOR An Officer who operates and controls the shipboard communication equipment.

RAISON D'ETAT (French) The reason of state. Decision superseding all else.

R&CC Riots and Civil Commotion.

RATTANS Long trailing stems of various species of palms. When split, used for caning chairs, making rough brooms.

RCDS Raster Chart Display System. The electronic chart display in use by the British Admiralty. Based on an image of the paper chart it is far inferior to the ECDIS, and is not accepted by SOLAS to ensure the seaworthiness of the vessel so a separate set of paper charts must be carried and corrected.

RD Running Days.

RDC Running Down Clause.

RCC Rescue Co-ordination Centre. Unit responsible for promoting efficient organization of search and rescue (SAR) services and for co-ordinating the conduct of SAR operations within a SAR region (ALRS).

RDF Radio Direction Finder. Navigational instrument which was used to find out the direction of a radio broadcast. Although lacking some precision, it was very reliable when all the other means to fix the position were not available. Now it is mostly replaced by the GPS; only a few coast stations are using a kind of RDF working on the VHF channel to locate small craft.

REACH STACKER Transport and stacking device mainly used for containers (or large pipes). The RS can pivot the load and reach out into the second lane to pick up its load.

REAM OF PAPER 20 quires; 480 sheets.

RECAP RECAPitulation of the terms and conditions agreed.

REEFER Refrigerator ship. A vessel designed to carry goods requiring refrigeration, such as meat and fruit. A reefer ship has insulated holds into which cold air is passed at the temperature appropriate to the goods being carried.

REEFER BOX An insulated shipping container designed to carry cargoes requiring temperature control. It is fitted with a refrigeration unit which is connected to the carrying ship's electrical power supply.

REGISTER TON 100 cubic feet; 2.8317 cubic metres.

REINSURANCE A contract for reinsurance is to indemnify against losses which the original underwriter has suffered but not against gifts. The reinsurance liability is limited to the original insurer's liability under the original policy.

RELAY Transfer containers from one ship to another.

REQUISITION Process by which the state takes the use of possession of property or the actual property itself of persons who are within the control of government.

RESIN Residue after distillation of the oil of turpentine from the crude oleo-resin of various species of pine. Also Rosin.

RESPONDENTIA A loan upon the cargo of a vessel to be repaid (with maritime interest) only if the goods arrive safely at their destination. The lender must be paid in principal and interest even if the ship perishes, provided the goods are safe.

RESTRAINT OF PRINCES, RULERS AND PEOPLES Covers any governmental interference of a forcible character with ship or cargo whether such interference be by an enemy of the state to which the ship belongs or not.

RETURN CARGO A cargo which enables a ship to return loaded to the port or area where her previous cargo was loaded.

REVERSIBLE TIME Option for charterers to add together time allowed for loading and discharging relative to terms of a particular charter party.

RGE Range. Range of ports in which the cargo could be loaded: Le Havre/Hamburg, includes those ports and all those in between: Dunkirk, Antwerp, Rotterdam etc.

RICE A cereal obtained from marsh plant (in the husk = paddy) or also as 'mountain rice' (also growing on dry land).

RICE PAPER Paper made from the pith of the stem of a plant from Formosa. Used by Chinese for painting on.

RICHTER SCALE For the standard measure of earthquake magnitudes. It is named after Charles Richter of the California Institute of Technology, who invented it in the 1930s. The scale increases at a rate that is exponential rather than linear, making each level increment vastly greater than most people realize. According to Charles Officer and Jake Page in *Tales of the Earth,* a magnitude 8.3 earthquake is 50 times stronger than a magnitude 7.3 quake and 2500 times stronger than a magnitude 6.3 quake. In practical terms, this means that Richter magnitudes are largely meaningless to most. The Richter Scale measures only the magnitude of an earthquake at its point of origin and says little or nothing about the degree of devastation at ground level.

RIGA LAST A measure of timber consisting of 80 cubic feet of sawn deals or square timber or 65 cable feet of round timber.

RIME OF THE ANCIENT MARINER Poem by Samuel Taylor Coleridge.

RINA Registro Italiano NAvale. Italian Classification Society.

RISK The amount insured.

RMG Rail Mounted Gantry. Device to stack containers the same way as an RTG but restricted in its movement by the rail.

RNLI Royal Navy Lifeboat Institution.

RO Routing Order.

ROB Remaining On Board. Usually a list of the weights remaining on board: eventually cargo and consumables.

ROLLING CARGO Cargo which is on wheels, such as truck or trailers, and which can be driven or towed on to a ship.

RO/RO SHIP Ship or ferry with facilities for vehicles to drive on and off (roll-on roll-off); a system of loading and discharging a ship whereby the cargo is driven on and off on ramps. Equipped with large openings at bow and/or stern and sometimes also in the side, the ship permits rapid loading and discharge with hydraulically operated ramps providing easy access. Fully loaded trucks or trailers carrying containers are accommodated on the deck. This type of ship is highly vulnerable if water submerges the main car deck, for instance after a collision. Poor lashing of heavy trucks can also cause a dangerous list if some of them become loose in bad weather. Many Ro/Ro ships have capsized, usually drowning some or all crew members. BESMA, which was in charge of the IFSMA working group on Ro/Ro ships, still does not agree with the actual design of these ships.

ROSIN Name for resin.

ROSTER, LIST OF CREW The roll recording the name and surname, nationality, age, post or employment of all and each of the personnel of a vessel.

RP Return premium.

RS&CC Riots, Strikes and Civil Commotions.

RSVP (French) - *Répondez s'il vous plaît*, please reply.

RT *1* Radio Telephony.

2 Rye Terms.

RTG Rubber Tyred Gantry. Device to stack containers with a maximum use of available surface. Can stack up to 7 to 10 wide and 6 to 8 high. It can also move from one lane to another thanks to its pivoting wheels.

RUNNING DAY A constructive calendar day of 24 hours, commencing at midnight inclusive of (unless expressly excepted) Sundays and holidays during which the ship is running as opposed to working.

RUNNING DOWN CLAUSE A special admission in policies of marine insurance to include the risk of loss or damage in consequence of the collision of the vessel insured with other vessels.

RYE TERMS Sound delivered (subject to any country damaged grains in the fair average quality of the season's crop).

S

S for SIERRA   Morse = (. . .)

Flag = white background with central blue square. When hoisted singly from a ship it means 'Engine going full astern.'

SA Safe Arrival.

S/A Subject to Approval.

SABOTAGE Wilful destruction of property.

SAFE PORT A port into which a vessel and her cargo can go without danger from physical or political causes.

SAG To bend or give way from heavy weight; to press down towards the middle (sagging), opposite to hogging.

SAGO A granulated form of starch obtained from the pith of the sago palm.

ST ANDREW'S CROSS Used in packaging for transport. Means harmful – stow away from foodstuffs. IMO, Material Class 6.1, Group III (US).

ST PETERSBURG STANDARD A measure of timber being 120 pieces 12ft 11in by 1.33in or 6ft 11in by 3in = 165 cubic feet, 4.672 cubic metres, 1980 superficial feet of 1in thickness.

SALVAGE The operation to save a vessel in distress. The expression 'salvage' includes all expenses properly incurred by the salvor in the performance of salvage services.

SALVAGE LOSS A total loss less net proceeds. This occurs when goods are necessarily, by reason of damage through perils insured against, sold short of destination but unless the whole of the goods are lost and/or necessarily sold short of destruction, loss is partial not total.

SALVOR The person claiming and receiving salvage or having saved vessel and cargo or any part thereof, from impeding peril or recovered after actual loss.

SANDALWOOD Hard scented wood growing in India and the Pacific islands.

SANDFILL Sand brought on land by truck or by pumping (from dredgers) to bring the land level to the required height or to create new land space.

S&L Sue and Labour.

SANS RECOURS Without redress. On a bill, written by endorsement, disclaiming liability in case of non-payment.

SB Safe Berth. Broker and chartering term meaning that the ship cannot be in danger when berthed. Grounding is often a cause of the un-safety of the berth; current, weak mooring, and many other dangers can render a berth unsafe.

SBT Segregated Ballast Tank (MARPOL). Tank used exclusively for water ballast but which can be pumped through cargo pumps under certain conditions.

SC *1* Salvage charges.
2 Straddle Carrier. Device that straddles the box to transport and stack containers up to 4 high.

SCANTLINGS Shipbuilding: sectional dimensions of the various parts of a vessel, regarded collectively. Wood: small pieces of beams of wood less than 6 inches square.

SCOW Flat-bottomed American lighter.

SCUPPERS Holes in the side of a ship to carry off water from the main deck.

SCUTTLE To let water into a vessel for the purpose of sinking her. The water, in case of fraudulent scuttling, cannot be regarded as the cause of the loss. The cause is the fraudulent act which admits it to the vessel.

S/D Sea Damaged (grain trade). Also Single Decker.

SDHF Standard Dutch Hull Form.

SEABEE Sea-barge, a barge carrier design similar to LASH but which uses rollers to move the barges aboard the ship. The self-propelled loaded barges are themselves loaded on board as cargo and are considerably larger than those loaded on LASH ships.

SEABOARD The line along which land and water meet, indicating the limit common to both.

SEA COCKS Valves controlling the flow of sea water into the tanks and compartments of the vessel.

SEA TRIALS A series of trials conducted by the builders during which the owner's representatives on board act in a consulting and checking capacity to determine if the vessel has met the specifications.

SEAWORTHINESS The sufficiency of a vessel in materials, construction, equipment, crew and outfit for the trade in which it is employed. Any sort of disrepair to the vessel by which the cargo may suffer, overloading, untrained Officers, etc may constitute a vessel's un-seaworthiness. A ship is seaworthy if fit to encounter the perils of the voyage and to carry the cargo contracted for. The test is whether a careful and prudent ship owner, knowing of a deficiency, would have required it to be made good before sending the vessel to sea.

SEAWORTHINESS CERTIFICATE A certificate issued by a classification society surveyor to allow a vessel to proceed after she has met with a mishap that may have affected her seaworthiness. It is frequently issued to enable a vessel to proceed, after temporary repairs have been effected, to another port where permanent repairs are then carried out.

SEAWORTHY Statement on the condition of the vessel. It has valid certificates and is fully equipped and properly manned.

SEB Shipping Ethics Board. Project for a better overview of shipping issues by seafarers.

SECCOTINE A liquid substitute for glue.

SELF-SUSTAINING SHIP, GEARED VESSEL A container ship which has her own equipment for loading and discharging, enabling the ship to serve ports which do not have suitable lifting equipment.

SELF-TRIMMING SHIP A ship with holds shaped in such a way that the cargo levels itself.

SELF-UNLOADER, SELF DISCHARGER A bulk carrier which is equipped with gear for unloading cargo without help from shore equipment.

SEMI-SUBMERSIBLE Deck supported by pillars, fastened to pontoons. The pontoons are half submerged during operations. Kept in position by anchors or by dynamic positioning. Normally equipped with its own propulsion machinery.

SET The direction in which the current flows or of the wind or the tide.

SF Stowage Factor.

SGS Société Générale de Surveillance. Swiss surveying company mainly for verification of quality or of price.

SHAFT HORSEPOWER Used in connection with steam turbine engines.

SHALE Kinds of clay splitting readily into thin plates and resembling slate but softer and not so solid. Shale oil is generally a dark green colour and contains a large percentage of paraffin wax.

SHEA BUTTER A solid vegetable fat obtained from a West African tree.

SHELLAC *See Lac.*

SHEX Sundays, Holidays EXcluded.

SHIFTING This refers to movements or changing positions of cargo from one place to another. This can easily endanger the seaworthiness and safety of the ship.

SHINC Sundays, Holidays, INCluded.

SHIP BROKER A mercantile agent who transacts the business for a ship when in port and usually also transacts the business of insurance.

SHIP CHANDLER A tradesman who supplies the small wares and stores required for a ship.

SHIPPERS Individuals or businesses purchasing transportation services.

SHIPPER'S COUNCIL An organization of shippers formed to collectively negotiate conditions and services with the conferences of ship operators.

SHIPPING DAYS Number of days agreed upon by the owners and charterers of a vessel for loading beyond which demurrage is reckoned.

SHIPPING NOTE A delivery or receipt note of particulars of goods forwarded to a wharf or dock for shipment.

SHIP'S AGENT A person or firm who transacts all business in a port on behalf of ship owners or charterers. Also called shipping agent, agent.

SHIP'S ARTICLES A written agreement between the Master of a ship and the crew concerning their employment. It includes rates of pay and capacity of each crewman, the date of commencement of the voyage and its duration.

SHIP'S CREW

DECK DEPARTMENT (LICENSED)

Master (Captain) Highest Officer aboard ship. Oversees all ship operations. Keeps ship's records. Handles accounting and bookkeeping. Takes command of vessel in inclement weather and in crowded or narrow waters. Handles communications. Receives and implements instructions from home office.

First Mate (Chief Mate) In charge of four to eight watch. Directly responsible for all deck operations (cargo storage and handling, deck maintenance deck supplies). Assigns and checks deck department overtime. Ship's Medical Officer.

Second Mate In charge of twelve to four watch. Ship's Navigation Officer. Keeps charts (maps) up to date and monitors navigation equipment on bridge.

Third Mate In charge of eight to twelve watch. Makes sure emergency survival equipment (lifeboats, life rings etc) are in order. Assists other Officers as directed.

ENGINE DEPARTMENT (LICENSED)

Chief Engineer Head of engineer department. Keeps records of all engine parts and repairs. Generally tends to the functioning of all mechanical equipment on ship. Calculates fuel and water consumption and requirements. Coordinates operations with shore-side port engineer.

First Assistant Engineer In charge of four to eight watch. Usually works from four to eight, handling engine maintenance. Assigns duties to unlicensed personnel and monitors and records overtime. Consults with Chief regarding work priorities.

Second Assistant Engineer In charge of twelve to four watch. On steam vessels has responsibility for the boilers, on diesels, the evaporators and the auxiliary equipment.

Third Assistant Engineer In charge of eight to twelve watch. Maintains lighting fixtures. Repairs malfunctioning accessories in living quarters. Assists other engineers as directed.

DECK DEPARTMENT (UNLICENSED)

Boatswain (Bosun) Receives working orders for deck gang from Chief Mate and passes them onto ABs and ordinaries. Tantamount to foreman, he is on deck, directly supervizing maintenance operations.

Carpenter (Chips) Works together with the Boatswain on woodwork, tackle, gear.

Ship's Chairman (Shop Steward) In charge of union business for unlicensed personnel. Handles grievances.

Able Seaman (AB) Stands watch, during which he steers the vessel, stands lookout, assists the Mate on watch and makes rounds of the ship to ensure that all is in order. He also ties up and unties the vessel to and from the dock and maintains the equipment on deck.

Ordinary Seaman (Os) An apprentice AB, assists ABs, Bosun and Officers, keeps facilities clean.

ENGINE DEPARTMENT (UNLICENSED)

Pumpman And Electrician, Qualified Members of the Engine Department (Qmed) Trained in all crafts necessary for engine maintenance (welding, refrigeration, lathe operation, die casting, electricity, pumping, water purification, oiling, evaluating engine gauges etc). Usually watch standers but on some ships day workers.

Pumpman (Tankers) Operates pumps and discharges petroleum products. Maintains and repairs all cargo handling equipment.

Equipment (Liners) Maintains and repairs cargo handling equipment and also cargo with special handling characteristics.

Wiper Apprentice QMED. Cleans engine room. Assists Officers and QMEDs.

STEWARD DEPARTMENT

Chief Steward Orders food. Prepares menus. Assists chief cook in food preparation.

Cook and Baker (Chief Cook) Cooks and bakes.

Steward Assistant Cleans galley and mess halls, sets tables, prepares salads, cleans living quarters.

RADIO DEPARTMENT

Radio Operator Maintains and monitors radio, sends and receives messages. Often maintains electronic navigation equipment. This position no longer exists on modern cargo vessels as Deck Officers are trained for main communications.

SHIP'S HUSBAND The owner's agent who superintends the vessel when in port.

SHIP'S STABILITY The seaworthiness of a ship regarding the forces which enable her to remain upright.

SHIP'S TACKLE All rigging used on a ship to load or unload cargo.

SHIP TIME The mean solar time at the place where the ship happens to be.

SHORT SEA SHIPPING Maritime transport over short distances but sometimes reaching far inland along rivers.

SHORT TON 2,000 pounds avoirdupois.

SHP Shaft horsepower.

SIDE LOADER Lift truck fitted with lifting attachments operating to one side for handling containers or timber bundles.

SIGNAL LETTERS Letters awarded to every seagoing vessel and yacht to represent her name and so afford means of recognition by visual or radio contact.

SIGTTO Society of International Gas Tankers and Terminal Operators Ltd.

SILL OF A DOCK Upper edge at the bottom of opening into a dock.

SILO A grain store for grain or granulated material in bulk.

SINKER A butt log which has become saturated with water so that it sinks. Also: matting made of soft wood used as a base for dike construction. Also: piece of lead used on a fishing line ('hook, line and sinker').

SIRE Ship Inspection Report Exchange. Oil and product tanker inspection and exchange of information system. The main users are the oil majors, the charterers and the ship owners (Seaways A-40). This system did not prevent the chartering of the *Erika* by Total-Fina.

SISAL HEMP Fibre used for making rope. Not so strong or durable as manila fibre. Relative strength of sisal to manila is about 5 to 7.

SISTER SHIPS Ships built on the same design.

SIU Seafarers International Union.

SKIFFER (Swedish) Slate.

SL Salvage Loss.

SLAG Vitrified product of metals or minerals after fusion in blast furnaces; the scoria left after smelting metal.

SLEEPERS Pieces of timber, steel or concrete

(mono-bloc or bi-bloc) used in railways on which the rails are fastened.

SLING A length of rope, steel wire or chain with attached or spliced eyes at the end and used for lifting cargo.

SLOP TANK A tank in a tanker into which slops are pumped. These represent a residue of the ship's cargo of oil together with the water used to clean the cargo tanks. They are left to separate out in the slop tank.

SMC Safety Management Certificate (ISM Code). Certificate stating that the ship has an SMS.

SMP Single Mooring Point. Tanker terminal using a single buoy or fixed structure to fasten the vessel and carry out cargo operations. The ship can swing freely around this point.

SMS Safety Management System (ISM Code).

SOFT CURRENCY Currency which is not fully convertible.

SOL Ship Owner's Liability.

SOLAS Safety Of Life At Sea Convention. Main International Convention which regulates most safety aspects of commercial vessels.

SOPEP Shipboard Oil Pollution Emergency Procedure. Set of instructions to use in case of oil discharge. On most vessels carrying dry goods it is only needed for bunkering operations. These instructions, however, include many drills which must be carried out and recorded.

SOS Save Our Souls. Immediate assistance is required. Wireless signal of distress.

SP Safe Port.

SPECIFIC DUTY (USA) Duty levied on imported goods according to weight, measurement or number of articles, irrespective of their value. The long ton (2240lbs) is used in computing specific duties.

SPELTER Impure zinc, contains about 67% zinc.

SPONTANEOUS COMBUSTION Burning of a substance from causes inherent to itself. Also liable to occur when new coal is loaded over old in bunkers or when copra, jute and/or hemp are stored in close proximity.

SPOT (VOYAGE) A charter for a particular vessel to move a single cargo between specified loading port(s) and discharge port(s) in the immediate future. Contract rate ('spot' rate) covers total operating expenses, eg bunkers, port charges, canal tolls, crew's wages and food, insurance and repairs.

Cargo owner absorbs, in addition, any expenses specifically levied against the cargo.

SPOTTING Placing a container where required to be loaded or unloaded.

SPREADER Piece of equipment designed to lift containers by their corner fittings.

SPRING TIDES *See tides.*

SQUARE OF TIMBER One hundred superficial surface feet irrespective of thickness.

SQUARE YARD 0.836126 square metres.

SR&CC Strikes, Riots and Civil Commotions.

SRT Sinclair Roche & Temperley. Law firm located in London, Hong Kong, Shangai, Bucharest: ownership of shipping companies, chartering, carriage of goods, financing, insurance. www.srtlaw.com.

SS Steamship. Also Screw Steamer.

SSHEX Sunday, Saturday and Holidays Excluded. Method of calculating the lay days. These days are not counted.

SSW Summer Salt Water.

ST Short Ton, 2000lbs avoirdupois.

STABILITY The power a vessel has of righting herself when heeled over from any outside cause. The stability lever should always be positive ie the meta-centre (M) should be higher than the centre of gravity (G).

STACK CAR Articulated multiple platform railway wagon that allows containers to be double stacked.

STACK TRAIN Rail service whereby railway wagons carry containers stacked two high on specially operated unit trains.

STAITHS Lines of rails projecting over a river; a drop from which vessels can load bulk cargo.

STANDARD A measure of wood. *See Gothenburg and Quebec.*

STAND-BY VESSEL Stationed near an offshore installation, responsible for evacuating its crew in emergencies. Also performs continuous guard function, warning other vessels to keep their distance from installations etc.

STARBOARD The right hand side of a ship when facing the front or forward end. The starboard side of a ship during darkness is indicated by a green light. The origin of the word is from the Dutch word 'stuur' meaning 'steering device'. The first ships only had an oar fixed on the right hand side of the ship, near the after section. The man pushing and pulling the 'oar' held the steering device and stood with his *back* to the other side of the ship. This is the origin of the Dutch word 'bakboord'. As the position of the steering device sticking out on the starboard side was a hindrance for berthing the ship, the English preferred to bring the ship alongside the quay with the opposite side of the 'stuur' and called it thus 'port side'. In French the words are also the same, *tribord* from 'estribord' and *bâbord* from 'bakboord'.

STATION BILL A list which shows the vessel's complement and details their various duties in connection with fire and boat drills.

STATUS QUO (Latin) As affairs are unchanged.

STATUTE MILE 5280 feet, 1760 yards, 1609 metres.

STATUTE OF LIMITATIONS *See Limitations.*

STCW 95/98 Seafarer's Training, Certification and Watch keeping Code 95. IMO regulations on the minimum academic and training standards for Deck and Engine Officers. These were necessary to fight certificates delivered by totally unqualified maritime schools. Together with the STCW, the IMO publishes a 'White List' of approved nautical schools worldwide. Even those actual STCW standards are still drastically low compared to those of three decades ago. With these STCWs somebody can become Captain after only 24 months at sea; less navigation time than some cadets of the sixties had when they became Fourth Mate not yet in charge of a watch. Even European nations are now threatening to lower the standards, assuming wrongly that anybody is able to sail or run a ship provided some minimum training has been offered. This goes against the increased complexity of the onboard technology, against the variety and quantity of the dangerous and polluting goods transported and against the proliferation of rules which must be adhered to. Furthermore, some training establishments are urging the various national maritime administrations to reduce further the sailing time requirements by allowing '*virtual sailing time*' to recruits who follow some special training or simulator courses!

STEM SubjecT Enough Merchandise. Note accompanying booking an amount of cargo or bunker.

STERN The rear part of the vessel.

STERN THRUSTER Propeller built in a tunnel athwart ships under the waterline in the rear part of the ship to help sideways movements.

STERN TUBE The tube through which the tail-shaft passes outside of the hull.

STERNWAY The backward movement of a vessel.

STEVEDORE Individual or firm that employs longshoremen to load and unload vessels.

STEVEDORING The act of loading and offloading vessel cargo.

STEVEDORING CHARGES Fees for handling and stowing or unloading a ship.

STORES A general term for provisions, materials and supplies used aboard ship for the maintenance of the crew and for the navigation, propulsion and upkeep of the vessel and its equipment.

STO-RO Vessel with capacity for break-bulk cargo as well as trailer borne cargo.

STOWAGE The placing of goods in a ship in such a way as to ensure the safety and stability of the ship not only on a sea or ocean passage but also in between ports when parts of the cargo have been loaded or discharged.

STOWAGE FACTOR Cubic space or measurement tons occupied by one ton (2240lbs or 1000kg of cargo); 1 ton of steel takes up $0.2m^3$, 1 ton of grain takes up $1.7m^3$.

STRADDLE CARRIER Mobile truck equipment capable of lifting and transporting a container within its own framework (the equipment 'straddles' the container, in French *chariot cavalier*).

STRANDING The running of a ship on shore on a underwater obstacle.

STRESS *Stress* is force, while *strain* is permanent distortion due to some stress.

STRIKE Concerted refusal by employees to work till some grievance is remedied.

STRINGERS Wide flat iron girders alongside the side of a steel vessel in the main lower holds which run from end to end of the vessel.

STURDONS Port workers engaged in the stowage of cargo in the holds of a ship.

STW, STOW Stowage factor often expressed in cubic feet per ton. In scrap iron 'STW ABT 54' means 54 cubic feet per ton.

SW Salt Water. In reference to the water supporting the ship, meaning sea water. Usually the density of salt water is 1.026 but can vary from 1.023 up to 1.030 or even 1.033 in places like the Bitter Lakes in the Suez Canal.

SWL Safe Working Load. Maximum load that can be lifted by chain, wire or rope.

SUBJECT TO Depending upon as a condition.

SUBROGATION Where property is insured against loss, the insurers, after the insured has been indemnified by them, are put in the place of the assured with regard to every legal right of recovery he may have against a third party respecting the subject matter insured.

SUEZ CANAL TONNAGE Vessels navigating the Suez Canal require a special tonnage certificate as the method of computing the net registered tonnage differs in some details from the ordinary system.

SULPHURIC ACID or oil of vitriol. A dense oily colourless highly acidic and corrosive fluid.

SUPERCARGO A person sent with a vessel to dispose of its cargo to the best advantage.

SUPPLY CHAIN Logistics management system that integrates the sequence of activities from delivery of raw materials to the manufacturer through to delivery of the finished product to the customer in measurable components.

SWAD Salt Water Arrival Draught.

SWL Safe Working Load.

T

T for TANGO   Morse = (–)

Flag = red, white, blue vertical stripes. When hoisted singly from a ship it means 'Do not pass ahead of me.'

TAIL SHAFT The extreme section at the aft end of a ship's propeller shaft.

TALC A mineral which readily splits into transparent flakes. It consists of silica, magnesia and small amounts of lime.

TALLOW Animal fat boiled down. Obtained chiefly from sheep or oxen.

TANK-BARGE A river barge designed for the carriage of liquid bulk cargoes.

TANK CLEANING Removal of all traces of a cargo from the tanks of a tanker normally by means of high pressure water jets.

TANKER A tanker is a bulk carrier designed to transport liquid cargo, most often petroleum products. Oil tankers vary in size from small coastal vessels of

1500 tons deadweight through medium-sized ship of 60,000 tons to the giant VLCCs (very large crude carriers up to 350,000t) and ULCCs (Ultra Large Crude Carriers up to 500,000t).

TAR Dark viscous liquid obtained by dry distillation of wood, coal etc. Pitch is the solid black shining substance got by boiling down tar; it is semi-liquid when hot and hard when cold.

TARE WEIGHT Weight of wrapping or packing; added to the net weight of cargo to determine its gross weight.

TBA To Be Advized, Agreed.

TBN To Be Named, To Be Nominated.

T/C Time Charter. Also Till Countermanded.

T/C EQUIVALENT Revenue per day for time charter.

TDL Train Discharge List.

TEAK An Indian or Burmese tree. The timber is hard, heavy and durable. Used in shipbuilding.

TERMINAL Assigned area in which containers are prepared for loading into a vessel, train, truck or airplane or are stacked immediately after discharge from the vessel, train, truck etc. Also: area where passengers arrive or depart from vessels or airplanes.

TERMINAL CHARGE Charge for a service performed in a carrier's terminal area.

TERRITORIAL WATERS That portion of the sea up to a limited distance which is immediately adjacent to the shores of any country and over which the sovereignty and exclusive jurisdiction of that country extends.

TEU Twenty foot Equivalent Unit (containers). A measurement of cargo-carrying capacity on a container ship, referring to a common container size of 20ft in length.

THAMES MEASUREMENT TONNAGE Approximate representation of the internal capacity of a yacht derived from a system of measurement adopted by the Royal Thames Yacht Club in 1854. The rule for computing the TM tonnage is as follows: from the length (measured from the foreside of the stem to the after side of the sternpost or deck) deduct the breadth, multiply this result by the breadth and that product by the half breadth and divide by 94.

THPA Tees & Hartlepool Port Authority. UK port agency.

THROUGH BILL OF LADING Bill made to carry

goods including ocean, river and land transport where necessary.

THROUGHPUT CHARGE Charge for moving cargo or container through a terminal.

TI Transportation Institute, a non-profit organization devoted to maritime research and education.

TIDES Tides vary in height; high and low water alternate during varying periods (twice a day each, twice a month or year). Spring tides occur about twice a month about the first and the last quarter of the moon. Least extreme tides are called *neap* tides.

TIME BAR Time after which legal claims will not be entertained.

TIME CHARTER A form of charter party wherein the owner lets or leases his vessel and crew to the charterer for a stipulated period of time, within the geographical limits stipulated and for an agreed upon price per day. The charterer pays for the bunkers and port charges in addition to the charter hire.

TIME POLICIES Policies issued for a specified period in connection with the hull and machinery of the vessel.

TINPLATE Thin sheet-iron covered with a very thin layer of tin.

TITLE XI A ship financing guarantee programme.

TIV Total Insured Value.

TL Total Loss.

TLL Train Loading List.

TLM 96 Tolerance Limit Median value for 96 hours. The concentration of a substance which would kill 50% of exposed aquatic organisms within a 96 hour period.

TLO Total Loss Only.

TLV Threshold Limit Value. Refers to airborne concentrations of substances and represents conditions under which it is believed that nearly all workers may be repeatedly exposed for an 8 hour day, 5 days a week for a working lifetime. Expressed as parts per million (ppm) for gases and vapours and as milligrams per cubic metre (mg/m3) for fumes, mists and dusts.

TM Thames Measurement tonnage.

TNO Train Notification Order.

TON MILE A measurement used in the economics of transportation to designate one ton being moved one mile.

TONNAGE Expresses deadweight, gross, net, displacement. A quantity of cargo normally expressed as a number of tons. Formerly expressed only in register tons of cubic feet and without reference to weight.

TOPLIFT Attachment to a forklift truck that rises immediately when a load is lifted. To work inside a container a forklift mast should have 'free-lift' capacity = the forks can be lifted without the mast getting higher.

TOP-OFF To fill a ship completely where it is already partly loaded with cargo. Typically occurs where there is a draught restriction in the first loading port: the ship loads a quantity of cargo corresponding to the permissive draught and fills up at the second port where there is no restriction.

TOPPING-UP The introduction of inert gas into a tank which is already in the inert condition with the object of raising tank pressure to prevent any ingress of air.

TOP STOW CARGO Goods stowed on top of all the others in a ship's hold because of their relatively low density and the probability that they would be damaged or over-stowed.

TOR Time On Risk.

TORT Injury or wrong independent of contract, as by assault, libel, malicious prosecution, negligence, slander or trespass. An action may also be brought under a stature, eg a claim by a harbour authority against a ship owner to recover the cost of removing a wreck under a local act.

TOTAL LOSS Loss in which the insurable interest has entirely disappeared.

TOVALOP Tanker Owners Voluntary Agreement concerning Liability for Oil Pollution. Agreement between most tankers owners who agree to pay jointly for clean-up costs in case of pollution by oil discharge from one of their vessels.

TOW When one or more vessels are being towed; when a tug is towing one or more floating objects; to pull an object in the water by means of a rope.

TOWAGE Charges for the services of tugs assisting a ship or other vessels in ports or other locations; the act of towing a ship or other objects from one place to another.

TPC/I Ton Per Centimetre/Inch. Number of metric tons necessary to increase the draught by one centimetre/inch when the ship is loaded near the Summer Draught.

TRADING LIMITS Maritime limits area usually specified by range of ports in which a vessel may operate.

TRAMP LINE Ocean carrier company operating vessels on other than regular routes and schedules.

TRAMP SERVICE Vessels operating without a fixed itinerary, schedule or charter contract.

TRANSSHIPMENT Distribution method whereby containers are moved between large mother ships and smaller feeder vessels or between equally large ships plying on different routes and handing cargo over from one ship to another to complete the voyage.

TRANSSHIPMENT CHARGE Fee paid by the carrier to shift the cargo from one vessel to another.

TRANSSHIPMENT PORT Port where cargo is transferred from one carrier to another or from vessel of a carrier to another vessel of the same or partner carrier without the cargo leaving the port.

TRIM The relationship between a ship's draught forward and aft.

TRINITY HOUSE Association concerned with licensing pilots and having charge of aids to navigation, buoys, lighthouses etc in England, Wales, Channel Islands and Gibraltar. The principal pilotage authority in the UK.

TSS Traffic Separation Scheme.

TUG A small vessel designed to tow or push large ships or barges. Tugs have powerful diesel engines and are essential to docks and ports to manœuvre large ships into their berths. Pusher tugs are also used to push enormous trains of barges on the rivers and inland waterways of the US. Ocean going salvage tugs provide assistance to ships in distress and engage in such work as towing drilling rigs and oil production platforms.

TUNG OIL Oil expressed from the seeds of a tropical tree. Used in preparation of waterproof varnishes for aircraft and boats.

TURMERIC The tuberous root of a herbaceous perennial plant, a native of southern Asia. In Europe chiefly used as a dye and as a chemical test for alkalis.

TURNAROUND Time it takes between the arrival of a vessel and its departure from a port; frequently used as a measure of port efficiency.

TURN TURTLE Denotes a vessel capsizing.

U

U for UNIFORM   Morse = (. . –)

Flag = two white and two red squares. When hoisted singly from a ship it means 'You are facing immediate danger'.

U/A Underwater Account.

UBERRIMA FIDEI (Latin) The utmost good faith. Contracts said to require 'uberrima fidei' are those entered into between persons in a particular relationship, as guardian and ward, solicitor and client, insurer and insured and contracts of suretyship and partnership; though not strictly 'uberrima fides', they are, when once entered into, such as to require disclosure and the utmost good faith.

UECC United European Car Carriers. Largest short sea car carrying shipping line in Europe (1999).

UHF Ultra High Frequency (300 – 3000MHz). Apparatus using these frequencies is the best for internal communications on steel ships as it is not hampered by steel bulkheads.

UK/CONT United Kingdom or Continent within limits.

UKFO United Kingdom For Orders.

ULCC Ultra Large Crude Carriers. Tankers larger than 300,000dwt.

ULLAGE The level a cask or tank not quite full. Originally the quantity required to make good the loss by leakage or absorption.

UNCITRAL United Nations Commission on International Trade Law.

UNCTAD United Nations Conference on Trade and Development.

UNDER DECK TONNAGE Gross tonnage of a vessel less spaces situated above the upper deck when there are less than three decks or the second deck from below in other cases.

UNDERWRITING Subscribing one's name to a policy to become answerable for loss or damage for a premium. Good underwriting is not only putting a name to a risk but knowing when not to do it.

UNITIZATION Consolidation of a quantity of individual items into one large shipping unit for easier handling. Also used as an expression of cargo presented in one load: pallet loaded with cartons or cases, big-bags of one ton etc.

UNLOADER Automated port equipment used to unload ships carrying dry bulk cargo.

UNMANNED MACHINERY SPACES A space where alarm bells are installed on the bridge of a ship to trace or rectify any machinery faults. The computerized devices will report any fault immediately it appears so the engineers on board can attend to the problem.

UNMOOR Remove the ropes or cables from the bollards ashore that attach the ship to the shore.

UNSEAWORTHINESS The state or condition of a vessel when it is not in a proper state of maintenance or if the loading equipment or crew or in any other aspect is not ready to encounter the ordinary perils of sea.

UNSH United States North of Cape Hatteras.

UNSTUFF Unload cargo from a container.

US EFFECTIVE CONTROLLED FLEET That fleet of merchant ships owned by United States citizens or corporations and registered under flags of 'convenience' or 'necessity' such as Liberia or Panama. The term is used to emphasize that, while the fleet is not US-flag it is effectively under US control by virtue of the ship's owners and can be called to serve US interests in time of emergency.

US-FLAG VESSELS Registered in the United States and subject to additional US laws and regulations to which foreign-flag vessels are not. They must be owned by US citizens, corporations or the government and must be crewed mainly by US citizens.

USSA United Sates Salvage Association.

UTC Universal Time Co-ordinated. In the past referred to as GMT, also designated as Z.

UU Unless Used. Brokerage, chartering term usually accompanying the uses of Saturday, Sunday, holidays. If these days are used to discharge/load the ship they are counted as lay days.

V for VICTOR   Morse = (. . . –)

Flag = diagonal red cross on a white background. When hoisted singly from a ship it means 'I require assistance.'

VARIATION Error caused to the magnetic compass by the influence of the Earth (marked on the sea map with its annual change in minutes indicated as plus or minus).

VAT Value Added Tax.

VC Valuation Clause.

VCM Vinyl Chloride Monomer. Gas occasionally carried by LPG tankers. Highly carcinogenic, it is said that Germans allow a crew to carry the gas only once in their career. Classified as flammable, toxic and polymerizable.

VENTURE Term embracing the three elements of any commercial voyage, hull, cargo and freight.

VESSEL MANIFEST Declarations made by international ocean carriers relating to the ship's crew and contents of cargo at both the port of departure and arrival. All bills of lading are registered on the manifest.

VHF Very High Frequency (30 – 300MHz). Also designates the radio communication apparatus using this frequency. It reaches only slightly beyond the horizon, except in favourable circumstances where transmission up to several hundred miles is possible.

VISA Endorsement on a passport denoting that it has been officially examined and that the bearer may proceed on his journey.

VISCOSITY Measure of an oil's resistance to flow. Heavy oil of high viscosity flows slowly but a low viscosity oil is thin and flows easily.

VLCC Very Large Crude Carriers. Tankers between 200,000 and 300,000dwt.

VLCS Very Large Container Ship. More than 6,000 TEU.

VOC Volatile Organic Compounds. A general term which refers to a large and diverse group of chemicals, including hydrocarbons, oxygenates and halocarbons that readily evaporate at room temperature.

VOYAGE CHARTER A contract whereby the ship owner places the vessel at the disposal of the charterer for one or more voyages between specified points, the ship owner being responsible for the operation of the vessel.

VP Vapour Pressure. The pressure at which a liquid and its vapour are in equilibrium at a specific temperature. At this equilibrium the gas above the liquid is saturated with the vapour and condensation and evaporation are occurring at equal rates.

VTS, VTIS Vessel Traffic (Information) Service. Shore based system which controls the traffic in port approaches, pilotage areas . . . It is only efficient if experienced Masters or pilots are using the system.

W for WHISKEY   Morse = (. – –)

Flag = central red square set in a larger white square with all-round blue border. When hoisted singly from a ship it means 'I require medical assistance'.

WA With Average.

W&M War and Marine.

WAREHOUSE Place for reception, delivery, consolidation, distribution and storage of goods and cargo.

WATCH The day at sea is divided into six four hour periods. Three groups of watch-standers are on duty for four hours and then off for eight, then back to duty. Seamen often work overtime during their off time.

WATERLOGGED State of a vessel afloat but having so much water in her as to be unmanageable. A waterlogged vessel may be kept afloat by the buoyancy of her cargo.

WAYBILL Document issued by a shipping line serving as a receipt for the goods and evidence of the contract of carriage.

WB Water Ballast.

WBS Without benefit of salvage (usually contained in ppi policies and often 'increased value' policies).

WCSA West Coast of South America.

W/D Warranted.

WEATHER PERMITTING That time during which weather that prevents working shall not count as lay time.

WEATHER SIDE Side of the vessel towards the wind.

WEIGHT, WGHT Net weight is the weight of goods after allowance has been made for box, cask, sack or wrappings. Gross weight includes goods and package. *See Tare.*

WHARF *1* Structure built alongside the water or perpendicular to the shore where ships berth for loading or discharging. *2* Also: Mole.

WHARFAGE Charge assessed by a pier or dock owner against freight handled over the pier or dock or against a shipping company using the pier or the dock.

WHARFINGER One who owns or has care of a wharf and takes account of all articles landed thereon or removed from it, for which he receives a fee.

WHISKEY (Ireland), **WHISKY** (Scotland) Spirit made by distillation of fermented extract from malted and un-malted cereals, potatoes etc.

WHITE GOODS Cargo consisting of refrigerators, washing machines and deep freezers.

WIBON Whether In Berth Or Not. Meaning that the NOR can be tendered even if the ship is not yet alongside.

WIFPON Whether In Free Pratique Or Not.

WIPON Whether In Port Or Not.

WITHOUT PREJUDICE Leaving the question open. When a dispute has arisen and the parties correspond with a view to settlement, any letter marked 'without prejudice' cannot be given in evidence at the trial without the consent of the writer.

WLTHC Water Line/Top of Hatch Coaming. To see if the load/discharge gear is large and high enough to reach the hatches. As the size of ships has increased faster than the size of berths, this is often a problem. A ship can at times be lowered by taking ballast, even if one hold is needed, but the depth can be a problem also. Giving a list can help in some cases.

W/M Weight or Measurement.

WMO World Meteorological Organization.

WNA Winter North Atlantic.

WOOD PULP Made from various types of wood, the most common of which is spruce. Two kinds exist: mechanical and chemical. The former is wood fibre ground and crushed in water, pressed, rolled into sheets and baled in a moist condition for export. It resembles thick blotting paper and can be only used to make newsprint and other inferior paper. Chemical pulp is produced from wood by using chemical solutions (sodium hydroxide – $NaHO_3$), high temperature and pressure. It contains few impurities and is exported dry. It is made moist again to allow the fibres to float free and produce high quality type paper. Some of these fibres are also used in 'fibre enhanced bread'.

WORLD SCALE An index representing the cost of time chartering a tanker for a specific voyage at a given time. The index is given as World Scale 100, which represents the price in dollars per ton for carrying the oil at that rate. The negotiated rate will be some percentage of the index value.

WPS World Port Services. Joint venture of American Port Services in which Associated British Ports has a 50% holding and two Belgian companies, Cobelfret and Hesse Natie, 50% (LL 9-7Y). Working in the Port of Zeebrugge.

WR Warehouse Receipt.

WRECK The expression 'wreck' includes jetsam, flotsam, lagan and derelict found in or on the shores of the sea or any tidal water. It also means a leftover of a vessel ready to be scrapped.

WROUGHT IRON Iron which is malleable, produced by refining pig iron in a puddling furnace, the products being welded together in a plastic state without having been in a condition of complete liquidity. Forged or rolled, not cast.

WRTD Without Reference To Date.

WTBA Wording To Be Agreed Upon.

WTSBE Working Time Saved Both Ends.

W/TY Warranty.

WW Weather Working.

WWD Weather Working Days. Days during which bad weather did not stop the load/discharge operations. Often this is a subject of dispute. The stevedore can have too many goods on the berth and stop the discharge at the slightest rain. Regularly a record of the local meteorological observations is used but the crew had better keep its own record.

WWL Wallenius Wilhelmsen Line. Shipping company specializing in car carriers. President Lone Fons Schroeder.

WWSHEX Weather Working days, Sundays and Holidays EXcluded.

X

X for X-RAY Morse = (– . . –)

Flag = white background and blue Greek cross. When hoisted singly from a ship it means 'Stop carrying out your intention and watch my signal'.

XBE eXcluded Both Ends. Regarding the lay days, when an expression such as SSHEX is used, it is extended to load and discharge ports.

Y

● ●
Y for YANKEE   Morse = (− . − −)
Flag = diagonal red and yellow stripes. When hoisted singly from a ship it means 'I am carrying mail'.
● ●

YAR 1950-1974 York-Antwerp Rules Rules to settle general average claims as adopted by the Amsterdam Conference of September 1949. Their use is normally stipulated in the B/L or C/P.

Z

● ●
Z for ZULU   Morse = (− − . .)
Flag = four coloured triangles with their apexes meeting at the centre of the flag: black at the hoist, blue at the fly, yellow at the top, red at the bottom. When hoisted singly from a ship it means 'I wish to communicate with a shore station'.
● ●

ZERNOCON Old code name for charter parties relating to grain cargoes from Russian, Black Sea and Azoff ports to UK.
ZINC ORE CONCENTRATES A very heavy dust of the consistency of half-set cement. It usually contains 5 to 10% water, this being sufficient to keep the mass semi-solid. Cubage is 16.5 to 20.5 cubic feet per ton. When too wet (over 6% water) it can shift in the holds of a vessel resulting in a dangerous list that can even capsize a vessel. *See also Atterberg limits.*

SPECIFIC US TERMS

AID Agency for International Development in the USA.

AIMS American Institute of Merchant Shipping.

AMC American Maritime Congress.

API American Petroleum Institute.

ASBA American Shipbrokers Association.

AWO American Waterway Operators. The national trade association for the barge and towing industry and the shipyards employed in the repair and construction of these craft.

BLS Bureau of Labor Statistics, Department of Labor.

CAORF Computer-Assisted Operations Research Facility. A MarAd R&D facility located at US Merchant Marine Academy, Kings Point, New York.

CARRIAGE OF GOODS BY SEA ACT A law enacted in 1936 covering the transportation of merchandise by sea to or from ports of the United States and in foreign trades.

CCF Capital Construction Fund. A tax benefit for operators of US-built, US-flag ships in the US, foreign, Great Lakes, or non-contiguous domestic trades, by which taxes may be deferred on income deposited in a fund to be used for the replacement of vessels.

CDS Construction Differential Subsidy. A direct subsidy paid to US shipyards building US-flag ships to offset high construction costs in American shipyards. An amount of subsidy (up to 50%) is determined by estimates of construction cost differentials between US and foreign yards.

DOD Department of Defense.

DOE Department of Energy.

DOMESTIC OFFSHORE TRADES Domestic shipping routes serving Alaska and non-continental US states and territories.

DOT Department of Transportation.

EUSC Effective US Control.

EXIMBANK Export-Import Bank. A Federal agency that aids in financing exports of US goods and services through direct loans, loan guarantees and insurance.

FACS Federation of American Controlled Shipping.

FEDERAL MARITIME COMMISSION, FMC Authorized tariffs and rate-making procedures on conferences operating in the United States.

GOVERNMENT IMPELLED Cargo owned by or subsidized by the Federal Government.

HARTER ACT (1893) This US statute refers to merchandize or property transported from or between ports of the United States and foreign ports. Now partially superseded by the US Carriage of Goods by Sea Act of 1936.

JONES ACT Merchant Marine Act of 1920, Section 27, requiring that all US domestic waterborne trade be carried by US-flag, US-built and US-manned vessels.

MARITIME ADMINISTRATION, MARAD Oversees subsidy programmes to the United States Merchant Marine. Assigns routes to subsidized liners.

MARITIME SUBSIDY BOARD, MSB A branch within the Maritime Administration which deals with Operating Differential Subsidy and Construction Differential Subsidy.

MIB Marine Index Bureau.

MIRAID Maritime Institute for Research and Industrial Development.

MICROBRIDGE A system of through rates and service offered by a carrier for cargo shipments from any inland US location to a port, by sea to a foreign port and finally overland to foreign inland destination.

NATIONAL CARGO BUREAU A private organization having representatives throughout the main harbours in the US. It is empowered to inspect cargoes of a hazardous nature and issue certificates which are automatically approved by the Coast Guard.

NONCONTIGUOUS Domestic shipping routes serving Alaska and non-continental US states and territories.

ODS Operating Differential Subsidy. A direct subsidy paid to US-flag operators to offset the high operating costs of US-flag ships when compared with foreign-flag counterparts.

PERSONAL FLOTATION DEVICE Approved floats meant as life preservers and carried on board American ships.

PL 361 Tariff Act of 1930 Imposes a 50% tariff on maintenance and repair work done on US-flag vessels in foreign shipyards. Also, US-flag vessels must either be built in the United States or have been US-flag vessels for at least 3 years to be eligible to carry preference cargo.

PL 480 Agricultural Trade Development and Assistance Act of 1954.

PL 664 Mandates that 50% of government impelled cargoes be carried under US flag. Known as the 50/50 shipping law.

PR-17 Public Resolution which requires that US Government financed cargoes (Eximbank) must be shipped 100% on US-flag ships but that the requirement may be waived up to 50% in some cases.

TITLE XI A ship financing guarantee programme. If called 'Chapter 11' it represents protection against creditors.

US EFFECTIVE CONTROLLED FLEET That fleet of merchant ships owned by United States citizens or corporations and registered under flags of 'convenience' or 'necessity' such as Liberia or Panama. The term is used to emphasize that, while the fleet is not US-flag, it is effectively under US control by virtue of the ships' owners and can be called to serve US interests in time of emergency.

US-FLAG VESSELS Registered in the United States and subject to additional US laws and regulations to which foreign-flag vessels are not. They must be owned by US citizens, corporations or governments and must be crewed mainly by US citizens.

FINANCIAL TERMS

A

ABATEMENT Rebate or discount allowed for damage etc.

ACCELERATION OF MATURITY Declaration by a lender that the outstanding principal is due and payable immediately, together with the interest due, following non-compliance with loan covenants.

ACCEPTANCE Engagement to meet a bill. A bill so accepted. A bill of exchange that has been endorsed by a bank.

ACCEPTING HOUSES COMMITTEE, AHC Exclusive club of 16 independent British banks whose original denominator was their acceptance business.

ACCOUNT The balance of a customer's borrowing and lending with a bank.

ACCOUNTING PRICE Price used for accounting purposes only (not a market price). Often used synonymously with 'shadow price'.

ACCOUNTING RATE OF INTEREST, ARI Discount rate used to convert future values of benefits and costs into equivalent present values.

ACID-TEST, LIQUID, QUICK RATIO IBRD definition: the ratio of cash plus marketable securities plus amounts readily convertible into cash to current liabilities. Other definitions include:

1 Ratio of current assets less inventories to current liabilities.

2 Ratio of quick assets to current liabilities.

3 Ratio of cash plus near-cash assets to current liabilities.

4 Ratio of cash plus accounts receivable plus the market value of selected investments to current liabilities.

ACQUITTANCE A receipt in full for money due.

ACTUARY Calculates probabilities, usually for insurance companies that need to set their premiums according to how likely an event is to occur.

ADMINISTRATOR Type of receiver created by the British government's legislation on bankruptcy.

ADMISSION FEE Fee charged by a stock

exchange for applying for stock to be listed on the exchange.

ADVANCED REFUNDING Refinancing before maturity, to take advantage of favourable market conditions.

A FORFAIT The business of discounting instruments (like bills of exchange) that are used to finance export of capital goods.

AFTER SIGHT DRAFTS The currency is reckoned from the date on which a bill was left with the 'drawee' and the date must be shown on the bill.

AGENT BANK *1* Bank acting for a foreign bank. *2* Bank handling administration of loan in a syndicated credit.

AGIO The premium which the metallic or other currency of a country may command over legal tender paper money which is its face equivalent; the excess value of one currency over another.

AKA West German Company financed by a pool of 58 commercial banks in order to give export credits of more than one year's maturity.

ALLIGATOR SPREAD Any options transaction in which commissions eat up all potential profits.

ALLKONTO An all singing, all dancing type of account that combines money transmission service (cheques etc) with an interest bearing savings account and a loan facility.

ALL PURPOSE BANK *See Combined commercial and investment bank.*

AMERICAN DEPOSITORY RECEIPT A device to enable American investors to buy foreign shares without going abroad. The AD is a piece of paper issued by an American Bank which gives the purchaser the rights to an underlying share held by the bank at its overseas offices.

AMORTIZATION *1* The gradual extinguishing of any amount over a period of time (eg the retirement of a debt).
2 A reduction of the book value of a fixed asset.

ANNUALIZED PERCENTAGE RATE Standardized measure of annual rates of interest defined by British Consumer Credit Act. Designed to stop loan sharks misleading customers by advertizing 'only 2%' when what they mean is '2% per month'. 2% per month is 26.82% calculated as follows: APR = 100 (1 + rate) n – 100 whereby n is the number of payments per year.

ANNUAL RATE OF RETURN Normally this would be the net income for the period divided by the capital of the enterprise. However, with many government or quasi-government entities, it is difficult to ascertain the exact capital invested. In such cases the annual rate of return is calculated by relating the net operating income for the year to average net fixed assets in use.

ANNUITY BOND Bond which pays fixed interest every year in perpetuity, ie which has no maturity.

APEX LOAN Loan whereby IBRD lends money to an apex development financial unit which on-lends it to participating financial institutions which, in turn, on-lend it to industrial companies.

APPLICATION FOR WITHDRAWAL FOR DIRECT PAYMENT The standard procedure for a borrower to apply to withdraw funds from an IBRD Loan Account to make payment to a third party for amounts due.

ARBITRAGE Buying (or borrowing) in one market and selling (or lending) in another to take advantage of inefficiencies or price differences.

ARM'S LENGTH PRICE Price between corporations under fully competitive conditions (the opposite of transfer price).

ASK(ED) PRICE, MARKET PRICE The price at which a security or commodity is quoted or offered for sale.

ASSET A thing of value owned by a company or an individual. Banks have three different types of assets:
(1) Financial assets (the great majority) include their loans, bills and other financial instruments;
(2) Fixed assets are buildings or branches that are difficult to move;
(3) Intangible assets like goodwill and patents.

ASSET ALLOCATION Repartition of invested capital over the large categories of investment instruments such as cash, shares, bonds and fixed assets, not over individual titles or debtors.

ASSET FINANCE Mortgage backed securities and securitization of a range of assets such as whole loans, automobile receivables and other debt instruments.

ASSET MANAGEMENT The art of optimizing the return a bank gets on its assets. It involves finding a balance between the yield from the assets and their risk, maturity and liquidity.

ASSIGNEE Party to whom any right or property is assigned.

ASSIGNMENT An absolute transfer of property.

ASSIGNOR Party who assignor makes over his interest in property to another.

AT CALL Money at call is deposited by a bank or with a bank that has no fixed date of maturity. It can be withdrawn at any time when the depositor 'calls' for it.

ATM, AUTOMATED (automatic) TELLER MACHINE Computerized machine that processes financial transactions between financial institutions and their customers. It usually allows customers to withdraw cash, make deposits, check their balances and issue instructions for payments between accounts or third parties. Does not work with used currency notes.

AT SIGHT DRAFTS Drafts payable on demand.

ATTESTATION The legal act of witnessing a deed, affixing one's signature thereto.

AUCTION *See Dutch auction, Foreign exchange auction.*

AUTOMATED CLEARING HOUSE, ACH Clearing house that works with no paper like cheques but with electronic orders to debit and credit different accounts at banks that are members of the ACH.

AVAL Guarantee of the payment of a bill of exchange or promissory note with the signature of a third person appearing on the bill.

AVERAGE NET FIXED ASSETS IN USE, IN OPERATION The average of the gross book values of such assets, less the amount of accumulated depreciation, as valued from time to time in accordance with sound and consistently maintained methods of valuation, as at the beginning and the end of the year under review, less the value of work (or 'construction') in progress included in such gross values.

B

BABY BOND A bond sold in denominations of less than $1000.

BACK OFFICE The service that deals with all activities not directly concerned with selling or trading.

BACKSTOP Facility giving a borrower a standby

line of credit, either in the form of direct access to funds or by underwriting an issue.

BACK-TO-BACK-LOAN *1* Operation whereby a loan is made in one currency in one country against another currency in another country.
2 A credit opened by a bank on the strength of another credit.
3 A scheme whereby a bank brings together a borrower and a lender so that they agree on a loan contract.

BAD DEBT A loan that is not repaid.

BAIL OUT Provide emergency assistance to financial institution experiencing difficulties. Often used for assistance provided by governments to banks.

BAISSE A downward trend over a longer period whereby exchanges go down by over 20%.

BALANCE OF PAYMENTS A country's set of accounts with the rest of the world. Can be divided in two: current account, capital account and gold – and foreign currency account. The balance of payment is always well balanced. A shortage in the current account will be financed by a surplus in the capital account. If there is still a shortage the gold and foreign currency account will bring equilibrium. This means that the official foreign reserves of the country will decrease.

BALANCE-SHEET-RATIO Ratio based on figures appearing in the balance sheet.

BALLOON LOAN A loan repayment scheme under which the last repayment is larger than the previous repayments. In some cases, the term is used to refer to a scheme under which the whole loan is repaid at maturity. The French term *prêt à coupon unique* refers to the latter situation.

BANK BILL Commercial bill accepted by a bank.

BANKER'S ACCEPTANCE US and Canadian term for a bill of exchange which has been accepted by a banker.

BANKER'S DRAFT A draft payable on demand and drawn by or on behalf of a bank upon itself.

BANKER'S MARKUP, BANKER'S SPREAD Gross earnings margin.

BANK MONEY Money on deposit at a bank.

BANK QUALITY BOND Bonds rated in the top four categories (AAA, AA, A and BBB) and generally regarded as eligible for bank investment.

BANKRUPTCY Condition whereby creditors can no longer be paid.

BANK WIRE An automated information and money transfer system (in the USA), competes with *Fedwire*.

BARTER Payment for goods with other goods sometimes also called 'counter-trade'.

BASE LENDING PROGRAMME The lending programme of projects that will definitely be ready for the fiscal year in question.

BASE RATE The key lending rate of banks in Britain which acts as a yardstick for other lending and deposit rates.

BASKET An assembly of various currencies making up the total value of the currencies it represents.

BEARER BOND A bond with title to the bearer (ie it is presumed to be owned by its holder. The same as a coupon bond.

BEARER MARKET Market where the majority of instruments are in bearer form.

BEARER NOTE A note with title to the bearer.

BEARER SECURITY A security with title to the bearer.

BEAR MARKET A prolonged period of falling prices (a bear claws downward).

BENCHMARK Measure by which an investment portfolio is tested.

BENCHMARK ISSUE A standard issue of a security.

BETA Greek letter indicating the measure of systematic or market related risk.

BID PRICE The price offered for a security or commodity by a prospective buyer.

BIG BANG The events that occurred on or around October 27 1986 in the London Stock Exchange. From that date stockbrokers were obliged to offer negotiated commissions instead of their previous fixed scale. 'Single capacity' was abolished and foreigners are allowed to own British brokers.

BILL OF EXCHANGE An unconditional order in writing addressed by one person to another, signed by the person giving it, requiring the person to whom it is addressed to pay on demand, or at a fixed or determinable future time, a sum of money to, or to the order of, a specified person or to bearer.

BILL OF LADING Document giving title to goods in transit. It has a brief description of the goods and where they are to be delivered.

BILLS RECEIVABLE Unpaid bills claimable by an individual or firm.

BISQUE CLAUSE Clause in loan agreement that entitles a borrower to postpone payments of interest and principal for limited periods of time in balance of payment difficulties.

BLEND COUNTRY Country eligible to receive financing from IBRD or IDA.

BLENDED GRANT ELEMENT Grant element for a blend country receiving both IBRD loans and IDA credit.

BLENDED INTEREST RATE Combined interest rate for a blend country receiving IBRD loan and IDA credit.

BLEND FINANCING Financing from both IBRD and IDA.

'B' LOAN Loan made by the World Bank involving co-financing.

BLOCKBUSTER A product whereby the total volume reaches 1 billion US$.

BLOCK TRADING Trading in big blocks of shares. In the New York stock exchange any deal of more than 10,000 shares is a block trade. The alternative is 'selling in dribbles'.

BLUE CHIP Share or security of top rated corporation.

BOND Paper issued by a company or government promising to repay borrowed money at a prescribed rate of interest to the holder of the paper. Debt instrument with maturity of longer than one year. US bonds are usually secured while UK and Euro bonds are usually not secured.

BOND ANTICIPATION NOTE, BAN Short-term borrowing that serves as an interim source of funds for a project that is eventually to be financed by the sale of bonds.

BOND CERTIFICATE Certificate given to the holder of a registered security.

BONUS SHARE A share given as a bonus to purchasers of such shares.

BOOK VALUE The net amount at which an asset appears on the books of account.

BORDER PRICE Price of a tradable good at a country's border or port of entry.

BORROWING RATE *See Interest.*

BOTTOM LINE The net result or net profit after all expenses.

BOY Beginning of the year. Used in financial and business-planning.

BREAK-EVEN POINT Stock market: point where two strategies are equivalent. Normal: where cost and sale value are the same and no profit is made.

BREAK-UP VALUE The market value of all the individual parts of a firm if the firm was to be broken up and the individual parts operated independently.

BRIDGING LOAN Loan to span from here to there, ie short term temporary bank loan to tide a borrower over until money promised from elsewhere is forthcoming.

BROKER Person who acts as intermediary between buyer and seller in securities transactions, thus a stockbroker, an insurance broker or a tea broker.

BROKER LOAN Funds borrowed by a broker, mainly from banks, for purchasing securities for customers on margin or other reason.

BROKER LOAN RATE The rate banks charge to securities dealers and brokers on loans made with stock as collateral.

BUDGET ACCOUNT Account designed to help individuals to budget for big, bothersome bills. Regular payments into the account per month allow the account holder to make obligatory payments during the year, even though that may leave him overdrawn for long periods of time.

BULLDOG BOND Bond denominated in sterling but issued by a non-British borrower.

BULLET (ISSUE) An issue to be repaid in a lump sum at the end of its term rather than gradually.

BULLET MATURITY Maturity requiring the entire payment to be made, rather than gradual payments over the life of the loan.

BULL MARKET A longer period of rising market whereby shares rise by 20%.

BUNNY BOND A bond that permits investors to reinvest the interest income into bonds with the same terms and conditions as the host bond.

BUYBACK OF OWN SHARES Interesting operation for shareholders. When a company buys its own shares back, decreases the total amount of shares in the running with the result that profit has to be shared by less shareholders and thereby the profit per share increases.

BUYER CREDIT Medium to long-term loan to the foreign buyer of exported goods. The loan is given by the exporter's bank and usually carries the guarantee of the exporter's national export credit agency.

BUYING RATE The price that a buyer will pay for a security.

C

CALLABLE BOND Bond that can be redeemed by the issuer before the scheduled maturity. Usually called when interest rates fall so much that the issuer can save money by floating new bonds at lower rates.

CALL A GUARANTEE Demand that a guarantee be paid.

CALLED BOND A bond called before the scheduled maturity.

CALL LOAN A loan on a demand basis (ie which either the borrower or lender may terminate at will).

CALL MONEY, DAY-TO-DAY MONEY, DEMAND MONEY, MONEY AT CALL Money deposited in an interest bearing account that can be called by the depositor at a day's notice.

CALL MONEY RATE, CALL LOAN RATE The interest charged by banks for call loans.

CALL OF MORE, CM The right to call again for the same amount of goods previously bought.

CALL OPTION Option to purchase designated securities at a predetermined price within a specified time limit.

CALL PREMIUM The amount over the issue price when a bond is redeemed.

CANCELLATION (of a debt) Voiding a debt by annulling or paying it.

CAP An upper limit price or cost.

CAPITAL Money used to run a business; a vague term made precise by the addition of a qualifying adjective, eg working capital, paid-up capital (paid up by the shareholders), authorized capital (memorandum authorizing the amount it can raise), free capital (paid-up capital, reserves and bonds less amount tied up in fixed assets, equipment and investments.

CAPITAL BASE Total capital of an organization, ie capital plus reserves.

CAPITAL-DEEPENING INVESTMENT Investment aimed at increasing production efficiency and lowering cost.

CAPITALIZATION *1* Interest capitalization – market capitalization – recapitalization. *2* Total authorized par value of the stocks and bonds of a corporation.

CAPITALIZED VALUE Similar to discounted cash flow value. The present (capital) value of a future stream of income. To calculate the value by which the payments are discounted, ie the further away in the future they are due, the less they are worth now. The rate at which they are discounted is the expected rate of interest over the period, that is the income lost from not having them right now.

CAPITAL MARKET The market for selling and buying long-term loanable funds, in the form of bonds, mortgages and the like. Unlike the money market where short term funds are traded, the capital market tends to centre on well-organized institutions such as the stock exchange. Money market loans are generally used to fill a temporary need for working capital.

CAPITAL RATIO Banks' total assets may not exceed some multiple of their reserves and capital.

CAPPING Putting a lid on the rate of interest to be paid on a floating-rate loan. When market rates are below the cap rate, the borrower pays the cap rate and the extra goes into a 'rainy day' fund. When the 'rainy day' comes (when the market rates go above the cap rate) then the fund is used to top up the cap rate being paid by the borrower.

CARRYOVER Funds unused during a financial year which are transferred to the budget for the following financial year.

CARTEL Agreement among producers of goods or services to fix the prices of their products.

CASH Commonly, coins in the pocket and notes in the wallet. Cash can include a wide range of liquid assets that can quickly and easily be turned into ready money.

CASH AGAINST DOCUMENTS, CAD Form of payment used in international trade whereby payment is made on receipt of bill of lading.

CASH FLOW *See table.*

Cash Flow = Depreciation + Net result after Tax or CF = 4 + 9.
Free Cash Flow = Cash Flow minus reimbursement of principal of loans.

CASHIER'S CHEQUE A cheque drawn by a bank on its own funds and signed by the cashier.

CASH MANAGEMENT Control and use of liquid assets.

CASH MARKET *See Spot market.*

CASH SECURITY LOAN Security loan where cash is posted as collateral for the borrowed security.

CENTRAL BANK FACILITY, CBF (IBRD) A World Bank facility designed to increase borrowings from central banks.

CENTRALLY-MANAGED COSTS Costs that are the responsibility, for budgetary purposes of the institution as a whole, as opposed to those that are the responsibility of individual units.

CERTIFICATE OF DEPOSIT Certificate of an interest-bearing time deposit with a bank. Banks issue certificates as evidence of the ownership of the deposit. A certificate is negotiable and can be bought and sold on the secondary market.

CERTIFIED CHEQUE A cheque certified to be good by the bank upon which it is drawn, usually by the signature of the cashier or paying teller with the word 'certified' or 'accepted' across the face of the cheque.

CHAPTER 11 A piece of American legislation that provides troubled companies with protection from creditors while the company tries to sort out its problems. Also called *Receivership* (Britain) or *Vergleich* (Germany).

CHEQUE A bill of exchange that is drawn on a bank and that is payable on demand. Although electronic means of payment are on the increase in the USA and in Britain, cheques are still widely used.

CHEQUE GUARANTEE CARD A plastic card used in conjunction with a cheque book. It guarantees the recipient of the cheque that the bank on which the cheque is drawn will meet payment (up to a certain amount) regardless of whether or not the writer of the cheque has the amount of money in his account.

CHINESE WALL Separation between two parts of a financial institution that are not supposed to know what each other is doing because otherwise there would be conflict of interest.

CIF Cost, Insurance and Freight, an acronym added to the end of a price quotation to indicate that the price includes the cost of shipping and insuring the goods as well as the goods themselves.

CLEAN Refers to a money market operation without underlying documentary security.

CLEAN FLOAT Floating of currency where the value of the currency is controlled by the market rather than the authorities. Opposite dirty float.

CLEARING HOUSE An organization set up by financial institutions agreeing to initiate and receive among themselves electronic transfers of funds authorized by their customers.

CLOSED COMPANY A company in Britain controlled by fewer than six people. The company must also:
(1) Reside in Britain
(2) Have less than 35% of its capital held by the public and
(3) Not be controlled by another company that is not a closed company.
It then gets special treatment from the tax authorities.

CLOSED-END INVESTMENT FUND The American expression for what is also called an *investment trust*. 'Closed-end' refers to the fact that there is a limited number of shares in the fund, unlike an open-end investment fund (called *unit trust*). In the 'open-end' variety, new shares are issued every time an investor puts more money into the fund.

CLOSING PRICE The final price at which a transaction in a security takes place on a given day.

CLUB DEAL Loan whereby, instead of one bank being designated lead bank and others co-managers or underwriters, the various functions these carry out are divided among a limited group of members in order to save fees.

COFACE French export credit insurance agency. *Compagnie Française d'Assurance pour le Commerce Extérieur.*

CO-FINANCING Joint financing of projects in developing countries by the World Bank and other development banks.

COIN A piece of metal with a value and (sometimes) the face of somebody important stamped on it.

COLLAR A floating rate note with an upper and lower limit on the interest rate to be paid.

COLLATERAL The same as security.

COLLECTION RATIO The percentage of due and outstanding loans that have to be collected.

COLOAN A co-financed loan.

COMANAGER, CO-LEAD MANAGER Lender ranking next to the lead manager in a Euro-loan.

COMBINED COMMERCIAL AND INVESTMENT BANK, MULTIBANK, ALL PURPOSE BANK Bank offering a full range of services.

COMFORT Security offered in a commercial loan in the form of a guarantee or co-financing from a parent company, government or international organization. *See also letter of comfort.*

COMMERCIAL BANK, CLEARING BANK A bank that normally specializes in demand deposits and commercial loans. They are commercial in two senses: they make loans to commerce (for the financing of trade) and they are themselves commercial profit-oriented businesses.

COMMERCIAL LENDING Lending not always at market rate but under normal market conditions.

COMMERCIAL PAPER (CP), COMMERCIAL BILLS Promissory notes normally having a maximum maturity of 270 days, sold by companies or institutions to raise cash for purposes of working capital. Called a 'self-liquidating commercial transaction', like the export of goods.

COMMISSION The reward of an agent; the amount he adds on to the price of transaction that he carries out on behalf of a client.

COMMITMENT AUTHORITY The authority that

a financial institution has to make credit commitments based on the amount of resources it has received or had committed from donors.

COMMITMENT FEE, CHARGE Lender's charge for contracting to hold credit available. Payment for promises. A fee paid by a potential borrower to his bank to extract a promise of a bank loan when he wants it.

COMMON STOCK Units of ownership in a public corporation.

COMPENSATING BALANCE When a company borrows from a bank it may be asked by the bank to keep a certain amount in a deposit account in the bank. Why borrow if you still have something to leave in the bank? Probably this is to make effective lending rates higher than the legal limits. Compensating balances (which increase the total cost of borrowing) are very common in the USA and Japan.

COMPENSATORY FINANCING FACILITY A special fund set up by the International Monetary Fund to help member countries with balance of payments problems caused by temporary falls in the price of basic commodities (copper or tin) that they export and on which they largely depend. Since 1981 also used during erratic movements of staple cereal imports.

COMPETITION AND CREDIT CONTROL A new way of regulating banks introduced in Britain in 1971. It replaced direct control on bank lending with a package of measures including a reserve ratio requirement to all banks.

COMPOSITE RATE The way on which tax is paid on building society depositor's interest. The depositors receive their interest after tax has been withheld at the base rate.

COMPUTERIZED ENTRY OF OWNERSHIP, DEMATERIALIZATION Recording of ownership of securities on computer instead of on paper.

CONCERTED FINANCING, LENDING, CONCERTED LENDING DEAL Lending from different sources, agreed on by different lenders, usually in the form of a group of banks.

CONCERT PARTY A group of investors who act in concert to try to gain control of a company. Each buys a small stake, all of which, when combined, amounts to a controlling interest.

CONCORDAT Secret agreement among central bankers thrashed out in 1975 at the Bank for

International Settlements in Basel (Switzerland) referred to as the *Basel Concordat*. The aim of the agreement was to ensure that no part of an international bank's activities was left unsupervized. This is obtained by two methods, greater co-operation and exchange of information amongst national bank supervisors and more consolidated accounting of bank's business worldwide. The concordat was revised in 1983 after 'Banco Ambrosiano' has shown it to be full of holes.

CONFIDENCE The quality that keeps banks in business. The Wall Street Journal once said 'It is a truism that confidence is important to banks. That is why the early Hebrews did their banking in temples and the later bankers built banks that look like temples'.

CONSENSUS Short way of expressing 'The International Agreement for Guidelines on Officially Supported Export Credit', an agreement between 22 *Organization for Economic Cooperation and Development* member countries on how far they will go in subsidizing interest rates on loans to exporters.

CONSOLIDATION The combining of the accounts of a parent company with those of its subsidiaries. In Europe this is the exception rather than the rule.

CONSORTIUM BANK A bank owned by a group of other banks from a number of different countries, no one of which owns a majority share.

CONSUMER CONFIDENCE Indicator for the confidence and expectations of consumers in a country or region about the development of the economy. This information is collected usually monthly via standardized questions. It is used as a prophesy of future consumer spending and, thus, provides companies and the financial market an important element for the estimation of the development of the economic business outlook.

CONSUMER CREDIT A bank loan to a consumer to enable him to consume the sort of things you buy in shops and car show-rooms. Specialized government agencies are involved in ensuring that consumer credit is granted fairly. In the USA, bank credit cards are at the base of the high consumer spending that often gets consumers in trouble.

CONTINGENCY FINANCING FACILITY
Facility providing additional lending if specified
events or adverse circumstances beyond the debtor's
control occur.

CONTINGENT LIABILITY Liability that only
becomes a liability when something else happens.
Example: A guarantor becomes liable for his
guarantee only if the debt that he has guaranteed
does not get paid by the debtor.

CONTRACT FINANCING Project finance,
involving the use of commercial contracts such as a
ship charter or take-or-pay contract as security for
the loan.

CONTRACTUAL SAVINGS INSTITUTION
Institutions dealing with contractual savings, ie
savings that have to be made, such as pensions.

CONTROLLING INTEREST Ownership of a
corporation in excess of 50%. Also used for
ownership of less than 50% if the remainder of the
stock is distributed among many owners.

CONVENIENCE CREDIT Readily available credit
where no charge is openly levied. Refers in particular
to credit and charge cards.

CONVERTIBLE BOND A bond that can be
exchanged for shares at a certain time at the request
of the bond holder.

CO-OPERATIVE BANK A bank that is run as a
co-operative in which members buy shares.
Their money is then used to make loans to other
members.

CORE INFLATION The basic level of inflation
over a period of time (eg a decade) as opposed to
temporary fluctuations in the rate.

CORPORATE BOND Debt instrument issued by a
private corporation.

CORPORATE CHARGE CARD Charge or credit
card issued to the employee of a corporation where
the employer pays the annual fee and some or all of
the other charges.

CORPORATE RAIDER Person who acquires a
significant portion of a company's stock with a view
to take-over. *See also Hostile take-over bid.*

CORPORATE RIGHT Rights held by a partner in
a corporation.

CORPORATE SECTOR The business sector.

CORRELATION Measure between -1 and +1
indicating by how much two variables, as for two
shares, vary together in time. When the two
variables go up together at the same rate there is a

perfect positive correlation and the coefficient is +1. It is -1 when both go down together. When there is no link between the two then the coefficient is 0.

CORRESPONDENT BANK A bank that makes an arrangement with another bank to act as correspondent. More and more banks are now themselves multinational, thus decreasing the need for corresponding banks.

CORSET Popular name for a form of monetary control introduced in Britain in 1973 and abandoned in 1981. Usually monetary control concentrates on restricting asset growth, the corset concentrated on controlling their liabilities.

COUNTERFOIL Perforated slip attached to a cheque. On it are written details (to whom, for how much, when) to let the writer keep track of his transactions.

COUNTER GUARANTEE In a guarantee operation, a guarantee provided in addition to the primary guarantee by another guarantor.

COUNTER TRADE *See Barter.*

COUNTRY EXPOSURE The extent to which a financial institution has lent money to one country.

COUNTRY RISK The risk developing in international cross-border lending. It exists when a country does not provide the foreign exchange to repay a loan, even though the borrowing company is solvent and willing to pay.

COUPON A slip attached to a bearer bond which can be detached and exchanged for an interest payment or dividend due at a specific date. Also used to describe the nominal annual rate of interest which a borrower promises to pay the holder of a fixed income security.

COUPON RATE Interest to be paid regularly on the face value of a long-term debt.

CRASH What happens when a lot of banks go bust at the same time, as in 1929.

CREATIVE FINANCING Financing using unconventional means, eg special swaps etc.

CREDIT CARD A plastic card that enables the holder to buy goods and services and also to buy on credit. Most are issued by banks, some by retailers themselves. VISA, American Express and Master-card make them internationally acceptable methods of payment.

CREDIT ENHANCEMENT Increasing the creditworthiness of a loan, security issue or other instrument.

CREDIT LINE The amount of credit a business can get from banks when and if they need it. There is the 'agreed upon' line and the 'tolerated line' (when a company goes beyond the 'agreed' line).

CREDIT SPREAD The difference between the interest on company bonds and the interest on public bonds.

CREDIT STANDING, CREDITWORTHINESS The likelihood of a borrower to pay back a debt based on past credit performance.

CROSS-BORDER SWAP Swap between two parties in different countries.

CROSSED CHEQUE A cheque with two parallel lines drawn across it. Between the lines are written '& Co' or 'Company' or nothing. A crossed cheque must be paid into a bank account (any account will do). That makes it less attractive to thieves than an open cheque which can be exchanged for cash.

CUM DIV The opposite of 'Ex Div'. A share that is being sold together with a dividend payment that has been declared but not distributed.

CUM RIGHTS The opposite of 'ex rights'. A share that is being sold together with an option to take up a rights issue that has been announced but not yet completed.

CURRENCY MIX The proportion of different currencies borrowed or lent by a bank.

CURRENT ACCOUNT British expression for an American's checking account, (normally) a non-interest bearing account with a bank on which cheques can be drawn and from which cash can be taken on demand. *See also Balance of payments.*

CURRENT ASSETS In general all assets except fixed, deferred, long-term investments and other assets not realizable or not easily and quickly realizable into cash. Current assets would include cash, inventories, receivables and short term investments.

CURRENT LIABILITIES All liabilities other than capital (or equity), reserves and long-term debt. They would include payables (with a maturity under one year) and accrued expenses.

CURRENT RATIO, WORKING CAPITAL RATIO Ratio of current assets to current liabilities. It is the main liquidity ratio. It should be higher than 1.0.

CURRENT RESULT (profit or loss) Result before exceptional income but after taxes.

CUSHION BOND A high-coupon bond selling at a price above its call or optional redemption price.

D

DATED RATE Date from which interest is calculated on a new bond or other debt instrument.

DAWN RAID A takeover tactic of buying up to 29.9% of a company (the maximum allowed before a full takeover bid must be launched in Britain) early in the morning before the stock market has opened. Brokers get prior commitments to sell from investors, so that the whole thing is wrapped up before the market can catch a speculative whiff that someone is building up a stake in the company.

DEBENTURE Written acknowledgment of a debt and having prior charge on assets. It is generally a sealed bond of a company for a sum on which interest is due till the principal is repaid. It is secured on the assets of the company issuing. An ordinary bond is unsecured. When a company is liquidated debenture holders have a right to the company's leftovers before ordinary bond holders. Both of them have a priority over shareholders.

DEBIT CARD A plastic card which, when used in an automated teller machine or point-of-sale terminal, identifies the holder of a bank account and debits the account with whatever money the cardholder authorizes. Unlike a credit card, a debit card does not necessarily provide card holders with credit facilities.

DEBT Amount lent to be paid back.

DEBT CAPITALIZATION Conversion of debt into equity.

DEBT CARRYING CAPACITY The extent of the ability to pay debts.

DEBT-EQUITY RATIO Mainly used to describe the ratio of total liabilities to shareholders' equity (net worth). It can also be used to describe the ratio (relative percentages) of long-term debt to equity, net long-term debt to equity, total or long-term debt to tangible equity (= equity plus revenue plus capital reserves). Equity would include the capital invested in the enterprise plus retained earnings and other reserves including capital surpluses arising from asset revaluations.

DEBT FINANCING Obtaining finance by using borrowed money.

DEBT OVERHANG *1* The total outstanding debt. *2* The total debt that cannot readily be recovered by expected growth.

DEBT RATIO Ratio of total liabilities to total assets.

DEBT RESTRUCTURING Changing the maturity and/or terms of a loan.

DEBT RETIREMENT Paying off a debt.

DEBT SERVICE COVERAGE Net operating income plus depreciation, divided by interest charges plus loan repayments. This measures the cash generated by operations against the cash required to service the debt. The ratio should be 1.0 or better.

DEBT SERVICE RATIO The ratio of a country's repayments on its foreign debt to its hard-currency export earnings. Bankers use the ratios as crucial guides to a country's creditworthiness but by the time the ratios have been calculated (usually very long) the country is already desperately rescheduling its debts. The problem is that most countries first call on their hard-currency export earnings for buying vital imports, not for repaying bank loans.

DEBT WORKOUT The process of moving towards a satisfactory method of paying off a debt, including restructuring, adjustment, obtaining new money and servicing existing debt.

DEEP MARKET A very active market.

DEFAULT The failure to repay a loan on schedule. At that moment a bank can take legal measures to try to recover its money or to get hold of the underlying security backing its loan.

DEFAULT INTEREST Extra interest due on an Euro-loan if regular payments are late.

DEFEASANCE A company borrows the money and uses most of it to buy enough government securities in the same currency to ensure that the income from the securities is sufficient to match servicing costs of the borrowing. The securities and the borrowing are wrapped up in a trust. It all comes off the balance sheet and, if the company is popular enough (ie if it can borrow more cheaply than the country whose government security it bought), it is left with a profit at the end.

DEPOSIT ACCOUNT A bank account against

which cheques cannot be drawn and which must always be kept in credit. Interest is paid on the balance in the deposit account. Cash can be withdrawn from the account if sufficient notice is given.

DEPOSIT PROTECTION FUND Fund set up to reassure depositors that, should the financial institution of their choice go bust, they will get some of their money back.

DEPRECIATION The amount by which an asset's value is reduced yearly. It is also used to evaluate the cash flow of a company. Fiscal authorities regulate the period of depreciation. Also in pure banking business sometimes depreciation is called so because it is wasting away; for instance, a bank branch that owns a long lease will be worth less as the years go by.

DEREGULATION The process of removing legal or quasi-legal restrictions on the types of business done or the prices charged within a particular industry.

DEVALUATION A government-directed downward move in the value of its currency in comparison with other currencies.

DILUTION A drop of earnings per share or book value per share, caused by the potential conversion of securities or potential exercise of warrants or options.

DIRECT DEBIT An instruction from a bank's customer telling the bank to debit his account with the amount demanded by a named cheque. Direct debits are designed to make it easy to pay regular but varying bills (like gas and electricity) with a minimum of fuss. Customers do not like it though since direct debits take control of the cash in- and out-flow out of their hands.

DIRECT FOREIGN INVESTMENT Direct investments made by corporations of the country in foreign operations.

DISCOUNT Difference between price paid and face value of a bill, bond or other paper. Bonds (known as 'deep-discount bonds') are sometimes issued at a big discount to their face value. Also sell at a reduced price or reduction of the price itself.

DISCOUNT, TO Buying for less than its face value.

DISCOUNT BROKER A type of American stock-broker. He simply buys and sells securities as ordered. He does no underwriting, offers no investment advice and has no in-house research facilities.

DISCOUNTED CASH FLOW Method of calculating the present value of a string of payments in the future.

DISCOUNT HOUSE Unnecessary go-between imposed on the banking system by the Bank of England to distribute Britain's money supply to the money markets.

DISCOUNT MARKET Markets in short-term financial instruments. Through these markets the Bank of England fine-tunes the nation's money supply.

DISCOUNT RATE The interest rate at which central banks will discount government and other first-class debt instruments from commercial banks or the rate at which they will lend to banks with the instruments as collateral.

DISCOUNT WINDOW The 'window' at which central banks may borrow short-term (at the discount rate) to help them make an orderly adjustment to sudden unexpected changes in their loans (assets) or deposits (liabilities). The maturity of loan from the discount window rarely exceeds two weeks.

DISINTERMEDIATION The exclusion of financial institutions (like banks) from the process of allocating savings. Companies can rely on bonds and equity issues rather than on bank loans or governments can tap the personal sector's savings through the post office system rather than by selling bonds to banks.

DISTRESS BORROWING Borrowing in a situation of extreme need when there is no other option.

DIVESTITURE Disposition of an asset or investment by outright sale, employee purchase, liquidation etc.

DIVIDEND The reward to shareholders, part of a company's profit paid out to its shareholders. Dividend is announced at the annual general meeting.

DIVIDEND STOCK Stock which entitles the holder to receive dividends.

DOCUMENTARY CREDIT Method of financing trade. Banks provide the buyer of goods with the credit on the strength of documents which prove that the buyer has title to the goods. They are often called 'confirmed' by the corresponding bank. The cost price is a percentage agreed upon between the bank and buyer and is payable every three months in advance for goods whereby the delivery period is long.

DOLLAR LIBOR The LIBOR for transactions in US dollars.

DOUBLE-BARRELLED BOND Tax-exempt bond with at least two potential sources of repayment, such as a highway revenue issue backed by tolls and taxes.

DOWNGRADE A LOAN Loans lent to a country are given a category, according to how likely they are to be repaid. When a country looks to default, the loan is downgraded (eg to sub-standard).

DRAFT A written order for payment of money 'drawn on' or addressed to a person holding money in trust as an agent or servant of the drawer; a bill of exchange or cheque drawn.

DRAWDOWN Actual withdrawal of money allowed during a loan.

DRAWEE The party on whom a bill of exchange is drawn.

DRAWER The party who writes out the bill or draft. The drawer is the creditor of the drawee.

DROP LOCK Clause in floating rate note whereby, if the market interest rates fall below a specified minimum, the rate of interest is fixed and locked in for the remaining life of the loan.

DUAL CAPACITY The ability of the same financial institution to be both stockbroker and stock jobber (principal). The opposite of single capacity.

DUTCH AUCTION A competitive bidding technique sometimes used in US securities markets whereby the lowest price necessary to sell the entire amount of securities offered becomes the price at which all securities are sold.

E

EARNING ASSETS Loans and investments.
EARNINGS PER SHARE The profit of a corporation divided by the number of shares outstanding.
ECGD Export Credit Guarantee Department

ECONOMIC PRICE, EFFICIENCY PRICE Price reflecting relative value to be assigned to inputs and outputs if the economy is to produce the maximum value of physical output efficiency.

ECONOMIC RECOVERY LOAN World Bank loan made to assist with the economic recovery of a country.

EDGE ACT An American banking law passed in 1919 which allowed American banks to do foreign business.

EFTPOS Electronic Funds Transfer at the Point Of Sale. An electronic terminal at the shop's check-out point reads a plastic card from the customer's bank, automatically indicates whether there is enough money or credit in the account to meet the bill and immediately debits the account with the cost of the goods.

ELECTRONIC BANKING Banking transactions using computerized equipment.

ELIGIBLE BANK A recognized bank in Britain with sterling acceptances eligible for rediscount at the Bank of England. There are now many more eligible banks including non-British.

ELIGIBLE LIABILITIES The deposits of banks that count towards their reserve ratios.

ENDORSEMENT The signature at the back of a cheque (or similar financial instrument) which transfers ownership from the signatory to the bearer. A bearer instrument (such as an open cheque) does not need endorsement.

ENTREPOT, TURNTABLE Banks operating as intermediaries between borrowers and lenders located in foreign countries.

EOY End of year (financial and business-planning).

EQUITY The part of a company's capital belonging to shareholders. On the balance sheet it is what is left over when all the company's liabilities have been deducted from its assets except the liabilities due to shareholders. In Britain shares are themselves often referred to as equities.

EQUITY LOAN Loan in the form of equity participation.

EQUITY MARKET The market in stocks and shares.

EQUITY PARTICIPATION Some continental European banks have taken equity stakes in their corporate customers.

ESCROW ACCOUNT A bank account held by a third party on behalf of two others.

EUROBOND A bond issued in a currency other than that of the market or markets in which it is sold. The issue is handled by an international syndicate.

EUROCLEAR A clearing system for international bonds in Brussels on behalf of more than 100 banks that own it.

EURODOLLAR A dollar deposited by a person or bank not resident in the US and held outside the US.

EUROMARKET General word for the Eurobond and the Euro-loan markets. Euro-loans are loans of Eurodollars and of other Eurocurrencies.

EUROPEAN CURRENCY UNIT, ECU Artificial currency, predecessor of the Euro, rather like the *special drawing rights.*

EUROPEAN ECONOMIC COMMUNITY, EEC Formed by the Treaty of Rome in 1958 with six original members, Belgium, France, Netherlands, Italy, Luxembourg and West Germany. Later Britain, Denmark, Greece, Ireland, Spain and Portugal joined. Since 2004 10 more, mostly East European countries, have also joined. Even more countries have joined since and others are on the waiting list. The aim is to establish free movement of capital, labour and services throughout the member states.

EUROPEAN FREE TRADE ASSOCIATION, EFTA Sort of compensation for Western European countries which could not (or did not want to) get into the European Economic Community. EFTA was set up in 1960 by Britain, Denmark, Austria, Norway, Sweden, Switzerland and Portugal, later joined by Iceland and Finland. Britain and Denmark left EFTA in 1972 prior to joining the EEC. Portugal left in 1985.

EURO-TREASURIES Exotic invention in the Eurobond market: it is a security which entitles the holder to buy a particular US treasury Bond at a fixed price and at any time within a given period.

EVEN ROLL Refunding, where approximately the same amount of debt is being issued for the old debt.

EVENT RISK Situation occurring when the credit standing of a corporation changes because of certain events (eg merger, acquisition, leveraged buy-out). Some corporations are subject to event risk because they are exposed in a specific area (eg political changes for corporations exposed in a certain country, climatic changes for corporations depending on a specific crop).

EX DIV A 'nota bene' added to the quoted price of shares to indicate that the shares are being offered exclusive of dividend payment that is to be made.

EX NEW (or EX RIGHTS) Note next to a share price to indicate that the share is being sold without the benefit of rights issue that has been announced but not yet taken up.

EXPORT ADJUSTMENT LOAN, EAL Loan made by the World Bank to assist a country to adjust its export sector.

EXPORT CREDIT A loan to an exporter to tide him over the time between sending the goods abroad and receiving payment for them from the importer.

EXPOSURE Amount of investment made, with the additional idea of risk.

EXTENDED FUND FACILITIES Special fund of the International Monetary Fund (IMF), available to help members who need to make structural adjustments to their economies. Medium-term loan facilities are granted to qualifying countries. The country draws down the loan in tranches, each tranche depending on the achievement of certain economic targets agreed upon in advance.

EXTENDABLE BOND Bond where bearer can postpone maturity beyond normal maturity date.

EXTENSION FEE Supplementary fee payable to lender of a loan extended beyond original period.

EXTERNAL BOND ISSUE Issue of bonds in a foreign country.

EXTERNALIZATION (of debt service payments) Purchase of foreign exchange needed for debt service payments.

EXTRAORDINARY GENERAL MEETING, EGM A special meeting of a company's shareholders called, in addition to the regular (compulsory) annual meeting, to discuss something out of the ordinary.

F

FACE THE MARKET To act directly in the market, as opposed to through an agent.

FACE VALUE, PAR VALUE The value on the face of a financial asset.

FACTORING Getting someone else to collect your debts. A company will sell receivables to a factor (often a subsidiary of a bank) at a discount. The factor then sets out to collect the money owed. His profit comes from collecting more than the discounted price he has paid for the debt. The benefit from the company which employs the factor comes from the improvement in its cash in-flow that results from receiving earlier payment.

FADE-OUT AGREEEMENT, PHASE-IN AGREEMENT A type of joint venture agreement where the foreign investor initially has an equity participation of more than 50% but gradually transfers this equity till the local parties have majority participation.

FANNIE MAE The name given to the Federal National Mortgage Association (FNMA), a semi-public body that bundles mortgages of American *thrifts*, guarantees them and then issues securities backed by them.

FAST TRACK COUNTRY Country with high level of investment and growth.

FEDERAL RESERVE SYSTEM The central banking system of the US.

FED FUNDS RATE Rate at which banks in America will lend each other their surplus reserves, ie the non-interest-bearing deposits that they hold with the Federal Reserve board over and above what they need to meet their reserve asset ratios. These funds are also called prostitute money, held for just one night.

FEDWIRE Automated information and money transfer system in the USA linking up its various federal reserve banks, the Treasury and some member banks. Fedwire does three things:
(1) It transfers reserve account balances from one member to another;
(2) It gives instructions about transfer of government securities;

(3) It transmits administrative and research information among its members.

FIA Full interest admitted.

FIDUCIARY DEPOSITS A Swiss specialty in which a bank takes deposits and lends them to somebody at the depositor's own risk. The advantage for the bank is that the deposits remain off its balance sheet while it still makes a turn on the transaction. The advantage for the depositor is a higher interest rate and the veil of Swiss secrecy. Most fiduciary deposits are simply passed on to other banks to become straightforward inter-bank Eurocurrencies.

FINANCE FOR INDUSTRY, FFI Britain's long term credit bank which changed its name to 3i. 3i is owned by a group of British banks and the Bank of England (biggest shareholder). The original purpose was to fill the gap in long-term finance for small and medium-sized companies. It now provides long-term finance for big companies also.

FINANCE HOUSE Specialist companies in Britain (mostly subsidiaries of banks) which take in money from the money markets and lend it to individuals and companies for anything from one to five years to enable them to buy plant and machinery or for cars or fridges. It is usually more expensive than borrowing from a bank.

FINANCIAL CENTRE Any place in which, for historical or tax reasons, more than an average amount of financial business is transacted (not just banking).

FINANCIAL ENGINEERING Application of innovative techniques in major national and corporate workouts.

FINANCIALIZATION The holding of assets (eg savings) in financial form (bills, bonds, cash) as opposed to in the form of fixed assets (gold, property).

FINANCIAL MARKET Market for the exchange of capital and credit in the economy. It is divided into *Money Market* and *Capital Market*.

FINANCIAL RATIOS Ratios which show a corporation's financial structure. They include *liquidity* and *leverage* ratios.

FINANCIAL SPREAD Income from loans and investments minus cost of borrowing.

FINANCIAL SUPERMARKET Via deregulation any financial institution can provide almost any financial service. Banks can sell shares and insurance companies can buy banks. The new financial conglomerates (Shearson-American Express) are called financial supermarkets.

FINANCIAL SYSTEM The complete set of financial intermediaries involved in passing money and credit around a country's economy.

FINANCING RELIEF The extent by which a borrower has his debt reduced as a result of debt reduction or restructuring. This reduces also his need to find new financing.

FISCAL AGENCY FEE Fee payable for registration of bonds and other financial instruments.

FISCAL DRAG *1* Reduction in real income owing to the increase in income from inflation, resulting in income earners being placed in higher tax brackets. *2* Action by public financial authorities with regard to economic activity.

FIX To manipulate a price. Usually considered nasty except when it is fixing of the London gold price twice a day (10.30 am and 3 pm) by five big gold dealers (NM Rothschild, Mocatta & Goldsmith, Johnson Matthey, Samuel Montagu and Sharps, Pixley). Johnson Matthey's bullion business was taken over by Westpac, an Australian bank.

FIXED CHARGE Security given by a borrower to a lender of a claim on specific assets of the borrower should he fail to repay. A floating charge is where the claim is non-specific and against any of the borrower's assets.

FIXED RATE Of interest or of exchange; one that does not change over time.

FIXING Quotation of the price of a commodity in the market.

FLAT Excluding accrued interest. A bond where the interest is included in the price is said to be traded flat.

FLAT FEE When a loan agreement is signed, fee payable in full by the borrower to the lenders in the syndicate.

FLIGHT CAPITAL Money that rushes out of countries when political or economic uncertainty make the maintenance of its value at home seem unlikely.

FLIGHT TO QUALITY In capital markets, the transfer of assets to higher quality securities.

FLOAT Money that arises in the accounts of banks from double-counting cheques that are in the process of being cleared. Double-counting is called float and has to be excluded from statistics that aggregate all banks' deposits. Cheques, drafts etc in the process of collection.

FLOATING CAPITAL That portion of the capital of an enterprise not invested in fixed or other capital assets but in current and working assets.

FLOATING RATE Of interest or of exchange, one that changes frequently. Rate determined according to the laws of supply and demand. In practice exchange rates do no float with total freedom. Central banks will intervene to soften market forces or governments manipulate their internal economies to give a boost to their currencies.

FLOATING RATE (NOTE) BOND, FRN or B Bond on which the coupon is established periodically and varies in line with short-term market interest rates.

FLOOR A floating rate note with a lower limit on the interest rate to be paid.

FLOOR TRADER Member of an exchange trading for himself.

FOB Free On Board. Used to indicate that a price quoted to an importer does not include the cost of insurance and shipping. Contrast with CIF.

FOOTSIE Name for the FT-SE 100 stock index introduced by the *Financial Times* on January 1 1984 and the London Stock exchange.

FOREIGN BANK Any bank operating in a country other than the one in which it is registered. Not that welcome when also trying to work the domestic markets of the host country.

FOREIGN BOND Bonds denominated in a currency foreign to the domestic currency of the issuer and sold in the domestic market of the currency in which the bond is denominated.

FOREIGN EXCHANGE AUCTIONS Auctions in foreign currency, as used in some developing countries, whereby the price obtained for the foreign currency at the auction is the rate of exchange applied till the next auction.

FORFAITING The business of discounting medium-term promissory notes or drafts related to an international trade transaction. Repayments are semi-annual and discounting is at a fixed rate.

FORWARD CONTRACT Purchase or sale of a specific quantity of a commodity, security, currency or other financial instrument at the current or spot price with delivery and settlement at a specific future date.

FORWARD COVER The arrangement of a forward foreign exchange contract to protect a buyer or seller of foreign currency from unexpected fluctuations in the exchange rate. A way of guarding against unpredictable losses on payments due in the future.

FOURTH MARKET (US) Market for large block sales of securities arranged by private firms.

FREE BANKING A fiction; there is no such thing. The expression is used to refer to a form of charging for currency accounts in Britain that imposes no charge for payments made from an account that is kept in credit.

FREE-LIMIT LOAN A loan which does not exceed the amount above which on-lending is subject to bank approval.

FREE RIDER A bank that collects full interest due on outstanding loans without contributing to the new money loans which provide in part the resources to pay future interest.

FRONT END FINANCING That part of the finance of a loan package provided by banks over and above the part that is insured by an export credit guarantee agency.

FRONT-LOADING SPENDING Spending at the beginning of a financial period.

FROZEN BALANCE A bank account that has been made inaccessible for some reason.

FULL SERVICE BANK A bank providing a wide range of services.

FUNDED DEBT The debt of a business or government in the form of outstanding bonds and other long-term notes.

FUNGIBLE The quality of which one individual specimen is indistinguishable from any other. Anything to be used as money (cowrie shells, beads or gold pieces) must be fungible.

FUNK MONEY See Hot money.

FUTURES Contracts to buy something in the future at a price agreed upon in advance. First developed in the agricultural commodity markets, potatoes or pork bellies. Futures have spread into financial and foreign exchange markets, deposits, government bonds and stock indices.

FUTURES MARKET Market where futures contracts are bought and sold.

G

GARNISHEE ORDER An order from a court forbidding a bank to release money that it holds in the account of A for as long as A owes money to B. B obtains the garnishee order and the bank is the garnishee. A few days after the order is given, the court has to decide whether A's account should be used to settle B's debts.

GEARING The ratio between the amount of a company's capital that is in the form of debt and the amount that is in the form of equity. Can also refer to the relationship between ordinary shares and *preference shares*. The expression 'income gearing' refers to the proportion of a company's profits used to pay interest.

GENERALLY ACCEPTED ACCOUNTING PRINCIPALS, GAAP Conventions, loans and procedures governing accepted accounting practice.

GENSAKI A yen repurchase agreement.

GENTLEMAN'S AGREEMENT An agreement which has no proof of existence but a cynic once said 'If a man tells you that his word is his bond, take his bond.'

GILT-EDGED Quality ascribed to British government bonds known as 'gilts'. Supposedly edged with gilt because of the low risk of default.

GINNIE MAE The name given to the Government National Mortgage Association (GNMA), a semi-public institution that pools mortgages issued by thrifts, insures them and then issues securities.

GIRO A payment system organized by a group of banks or a postal authority which allows customers of one bank to make payments to customers in any other without the use of cash or cheques. The customer fills in an instruction form which is passed through a central clearing system organized by the group.

GLOBAL BOND Bond issued simultaneously in the US and other markets. The World Bank issued this kind of bond for the first time in June 1989.

GOLD CLAUSE A clause in a loan agreement that fixes the borrower's repayment at an amount equal to the weight of gold that the original loan would have bought. When inflation is high and real interest rates are negative, gold clauses provide lenders with an incentive to part with their money in the expectation that the return will take care, at least, of inflation.

GOODWILL Extra that is paid by a take-over on top of equity and that takes account of image, trade mark(s), customer portfolio and growth potential.

GOODWILL CLAUSE A clause in the Paris Club loan agreement that commits the creditors to consider debt relief after the end of the stipulated consolidation period. In return, creditor countries ask the debtor country to meet two conditions:
(1) The debtor country must have secured debt relief from creditors not covered by the Paris Club agreement and
(2) At the time the creditors agree to review the need for further debt relief, the country remains eligible for use of upper credit tranche IMF resources.

GOVERNMENT DEBT INSTRUMENTS Debt instruments issued by governments.

GOVERNMENT PAPER Short-term debt instruments issued by governments.

GRACE PERIOD The period allowed in a loan schedule during which repayments of loan principal need not be made.

GREENBACK Slang for the US dollar.

GREENMAIL An anti-takeover manœuvre in which the target firm purchases the raider's stock at a price above that available to other stockholders. The funds for the purchase are often borrowed; other stockholders are ordinarily excluded from the transaction.

GREY MARKET Market in bonds that have not been given a firm price.

GROSS The opposite of *net*, a total given before any deductions have been made.

GROSS CAPITAL COEFFICIENT RATIO The amount of capital requirement per dollar of annual lending, equivalent to the average number of years a loan remains disbursed and outstanding.

GROSS COLLECTION RATIO The interest received less the prior year's recoveries divided by the interest received plus net non-accruals for the year. The ratio shows the amount due and annually collected during the year (excluding any amount collected but overdue from prior years) and relates it to the amount that was contractually due during the current year.

GROSS DOMESTIC PRODUCT The most popular measure of economic activity in a country is the value of total output of goods and services before deduction is made for the depreciation of the country's capital investment or for taxation.

GROUP OF CREDITORS Group representing the creditors of a specific country or countries.

GROWTH CONTINGENCY COFINANCING System used with the Mexico financing package, whereby special financing would be provided from co-lenders if growth failed to reach a pre-set standard.

GUARANTEE An undertaking by a third party to be responsible for a loan from a bank should the borrower go bankrupt. To be legally binding a guarantee must be made in writing.

H

HANDLING FEE, MANAGEMENT FEE Fee payable to lead bank for handling bonds.

HARD CURRENCY A currency that people want to hold because they do not expect its value to be eroded by inflation. The opposite is soft currency, the value of which melts away even as you hold it.

HEAD AND SHOULDERS CONFIGURATION Form of a bar chart analysis of securities which indicates the movement of a security up and down (or down and up) with three peaks, the middle one being the highest and thereby giving the chart the form of a head above a pair of shoulders.

HEADROOM The difference between the statutory limit on lending and the value of loans that are disbursed and outstanding.

HEDGE Security acquired to cover possible loss on speculative investments. Can also be applied in financial markets.

HIDDEN RESERVES What some banks are allowed to hide from the eyes of the readers of their balance sheets. It is done by valuing assets in their books at less than their real value.

HIGH NET WORTH INDIVIDUAL The sort of customer every bank wants: he earns a lot, travels a lot, spends a lot and needs a lot of financial advice and a lot of loans (which he is sure to repay).

HIRE PURCHASE A combination of hiring and purchasing. A person hires a consumer product (like a car) while he makes a series of regular payments. When the payments are completed the product automatically becomes the property of the hirer.

HOME BANKING Banking done at home by means of a television screen, telephone or computer.

HOSTILE RAIDER Corporate raider whose actions are not supported by the target corporation.

HOSTILE TAKEOVER BID An offer to purchase shares from a firm's stockholders when directors of the target firm have recommended that stockholders do not sell their stock.

HOT BILL Bill which matures at sight or whose maturity is less than the period making possible its collection in good time, necessitating immediate presentation of payment.

HOT MONEY, FUNK MONEY Short-term international capital movements motivated by interest rate differentials or evaluation hopes/devaluation fears. Since it has no long-term allegiance to any investment, its flow back and forth across exchanges can cause wild fluctuations in exchange rates, fluctuations that disturb central bankers who like to see rates move in an orderly fashion.

HUNG-UP ISSUE An issue which dealers have not managed to fully place.

HURDLE RATE A somewhat arbitrary rate of return, related to the current cost of borrowing money, set by the government or company to guide investment decisions. Below this limit investment is normally considered inadvisable.

I

ILLEGALITY CLAUSE Clause in a loan agreement which allows the lender to ask for repayment of his funds if a change in national legislation obliges him to withdraw from the loan.

IMMATURE INVESTMENT Investment which is not yet bringing in any returns.

IMPAIRED INVESTMENT An investment that has been reduced by losses or other distributions.

IMPLICIT SPREAD The ratio of the present

value of costs of the commitment fee and loan spread to the present value of outstanding loan balances.

IMPREST ACCOUNT, FUND An account or fund maintained for payments made in cash, commonly used as a petty cash fund. A fixed maximum sum is kept in the fund and, as the fund is depleted, this sum is periodically brought up to the maximum.

INDEXATION Maintaining the value of a financial asset in line with inflation.

INDEXED LOAN Loan indexed to the daily variation of the currency value due to exchange variations.

INDEXING, INDEX PROGRAMME A method of portfolio management by buying stocks that compose a well-known index, often the Standard and Poor 500, and sticking with them. (Not to be confused with index-linked, ie tied to rate of inflation.)

INFLATION ACCOUNTING The search for gold via historic cost accounting that has so far proved to be very elusive, the measure of a company's real performance in times of inflation.

INFLATION PREMIUM A premium added to a security to allow for inflation.

INFORMAL FINANCE Finance which takes place outside of the normal financial markets.

IN HOUSE FINANCING, SELF-FINANCING Financing from own resources rather than borrowing.

INITIAL MARGIN The amount a buyer is requested to deposit with a broker before commencing trading.

INITIAL PUBLIC OFFERING, IPO A firm's first offering of stock to the public.

INSIDE DEALING Trading in stocks etc by those who have advance notice of likely change in the market owing to their inside knowledge.

INSOLVENCY The condition of a company with liabilities exceeding its assets.

INSTALMENT CREDIT A loan that is repaid over a period in regular equal instalments. It is rarely used to finance trade.

INTER-BANK MARKET The market in which banks deal with each other is a very important part of any efficient banking system. Some banks get more deposits than requests for loans and vice-versa. The inter-bank market smooths out these imbalances by providing a way for a bank with too many deposits to pass them on to a bank with too many loan requests.

INTER-BANK OFFERED RATE, IBOR Rate of interest offered by banks for a large loan to the most creditworthy banks for a specific period and in a specific currency. The best known is the London one (LIBOR) but they also exist for Abu Dhabi (ADIBOR), Amsterdam (AIBOR), Bahrain (BIBOR), Brussels (BRIBOR), Hong Kong (HIBOR or HKIBOR), Kuwait (KIBOR), Luxembourg (LUXIBOR), Madrid (MIBOR), Paris (PIBOR), Saudi Arabia (SAIBOR), Singapore (SIBOR), 6 month SDR (SDRIBOR), Zurich (ZIBOR) and others.

INTEREST What is charged to the customers of a bank for the privilege of borrowing other people's money or what is paid to the customers of a bank for the honour of lending their money to somebody else.

INTEREST CAPITALIZATION Converting deferred interest payments into new debt instruments.

INTEREST COVERAGE RATIO Net income before interest expenses divided by interest expenses.

INTEREST LEAKAGE Changes in US interest rates due to movement of funds from the US to the Eurodollar market.

INTEREST PERIOD Period, during which an interest rate is fixed. At the end of the period the rate may be changed.

INTEREST RATE GAP A limit on the amount of interest that can be levied on a variable rate loan.

INTEREST RATE RISK Risk due to the difference in interest rates.

INTEREST RATE SWAP An agreement to exchange floating rate payments for fixed rate payments in the same currency.

INTEREST (Rate) SWITCHING Option in a restructuring agreement, which allows creditor banks to alter the interest rate base, either by having a fixed rate or a variable rate, linked to a specific rate such as LIBOR.

INTEREST RETIMING Agreement whereby the frequency of interest period is altered, usually from 3 or 6 month to 12 month interest periods.

INTERMEDIATION Process whereby a financial institution interposes its names and trustworthiness between a lender and a borrower. Example: instead of buying an issue directly from a corporation, an investor may deposit funds with a bank which, in turn, invests in the issue.

INTERNAL GROWTH Growth without intermediate take-overs or sale of assets.

INTERNATIONAL BANKING FACILITY, IBF International branch of a bank in a kind of internal free-trade zone, which allows banks to engage in international banking without some of the usual restrictions facing domestic banks. Those restrictions from which IBF's are exempt include reserve requirements, payment of certain insurance premiums and special relief from state tax.

INTRINSIC VALUE Value of an enterprise based on its actual (exchange) value of its possessions.

INVESTMANT BANK (US), MERCHANT BANK (UK) Institution that accepts new issues of stocks from a corporation and attempts to sell them to the public at a profit. The bank provides long-term loans and/or equity capital to industry.

INVESTMENT BROKER Person who acts as intermediary between investors and financial markets.

INVESTMENT CERTIFICATE A non-voting share issued by enterprises but which receives the same dividend.

INVESTMENT COMPANY (FUND) Company that uses its capital to invest in other companies. Two types exist, open-end investment and closed-end investment companies.

INVESTMENT GRADE PAPER Issue of paper rated at BBB or above (or equivalent) by a rating company.

INVESTMENT HORIZON Period over which money destined for investment can be missed.

INVESTMENT LEAKAGE Various unpredicted factors that increase the cost of an investment, such as management fees, inflated equipment costs and non-arms-length royalties.

INVESTMENT MANAGER A professional investor who manages trust funds, pension funds etc within the general guidelines laid down by the trust itself. That leaves him a lot of discretion but this profession is amongst the most influential in the financial markets.

INVESTMENT SECURITIES Securities that are particularly suitable for long-term investment (eg bonds) or top-rated shares.

INVESTMENT TRUST A company set up for the

purpose of holding the shares of other companies. These trusts are useful to small shareholders who do not have enough money to invest in a wide-ranging portfolio. By buying shares of an investment trust, the shareholder can effectively buy a small part of all the shares that the trust holds in its own portfolio. Investment trust shares are on average worth 30% less than the market value of the shares they hold.

INVISIBLE TRADE Trade that never sees the inside of a container but earns foreign exchange nevertheless. Services like banking, insurance and tourism make up the biggest part of invisible trade.

INVOLUNTARY LENDING Lending by banks as long as the resulting reduction in probability of default, multiplied by the existing exposure, exceeds the amount of new money multiplied by the remaining probability of default even after the new assistance.

INWARD SWAP Spot sale of foreign exchange and forward repurchase of some foreign currency against domestic currency.

INWARD SWITCHING External funding by banks for domestic lending.

ISSUE The process of selling new securities (bonds or shares). New issues can be made through:
(1) An offer for sale in which the issuing house buys the securities from a company and sells them to the public, or
(2) Through a direct sale by the company itself, or
(3) Through a private placement with a limited number of investors.

ISSUE PRICE The price at which shares or bonds are first issued to the public. This may not be the same as the nominal price which is on the face of the securities.

ISSUER Body that puts out new securities.

ISSUING CALENDAR Compulsory timetable for issue of new securities.

ISSUING HOUSE A number of large London merchant banks that do most of the sponsoring and underwriting of new capital by British companies. In 1945 they were formed into a City Club called the Issuing Houses Association. Its membership overlaps somewhat with the even more exclusive Accepting Houses Committee.

J

JEOPARDY CLAUSE, DISASTER CLAUSE, BREAK CLAUSE A clause in a Euro-currency agreement specifying that, if certain events curtail the lender's activity or the operation of the Euro-markets, other designated actions will come into effect.

JEOPARDY LOAN Terms indicate that a loan has serious problems expecting to make a loss (not necessarily 100%).

JOBBER A broker on the London Stock Exchange acting on his own behalf. Since 1986 the separation between jobbers and brokers has ended.

JOBBER'S TURN Where the jobber makes his profit: the difference between the price he pays for the securities that he buys and the price he gets when he sells.

JOINT FINANCING Disbursement by two lenders for the same parts of the project in a fixed ratio.

JUMBO BORROWING Borrowing in large quantities (usually in excess of $250,000).

JUNIOR DEBT Debt which, in case of liquidation, cannot be paid till payments on other obligations have been made. Opposite senior debt.

JUNK BOND, SPECULATIVE GRADE BOND High-yield, low-rated security. Used as a new way of raising money quickly as they attract investors who like the high yields and are willing to accept increased risks. The ratings are below 'investment grade'. Junk can be either high-class bonds that have fallen on hard times or high-risk bonds that are issued with a low rating.

K

KAFFIRS The shares of South African gold mine companies.

KEY INTEREST RATES The main interest rates, includes LIBOR, US prime rate, US federal funds rate and others depending on where they are used.

KEY MONEY RATE, CENTRAL RATE Term used to describe the main interest rate set by the central bank (or equivalent) and which effectively governs other market interest rate (in the US this is the *fed funds rate*).

KIWI BOND Bond issued in New Zealand dollars on the New Zealand market by non New Zealand borrowers.

L

LANDESBANK Regional banks in Germany that act as mini-central banks for the host of powerful savings banks. Have now developed into international lending and commercial banking specialties.

LARGE EXPOSURE BANK Bank with a large amount of outstanding loans.

LAUNDERING Pejorative word with connotations similar to 'white-wash'. The process of passing money through a very secret sieve or through a series of complicated transactions that disguise its true origin or purpose from tax control, fraud squad.

LAYERING Mismatching maturities in order to improve liquidity.

LDC Less developed country.

LEAD BANK, LEAD MANAGER Bank with main responsibility for arranging a bond issue.

LEAKAGE *See interest leakage, investment leakage.*

LEASING The hiring of capital goods or equipment to avoid the all-at-once cost of buying them.

LEGAL TENDER A method of payment that, by law, must be accepted as settlement of a debt.

LENDER OF LAST RESORT One of the major functions and major raison d'être for a modern central bank, whereby the bank has to provide liquid assets to the banking system when the existing liquid assets of the banking system threaten to deplete.

LENDER OF RECORD Lender that has the official commitment for a loan.

LENDING AUTHORITY The amount of money that the bank can lend, based on its paid-in capital.

LENDING CEILING The maximum amount that an organization can lend.

LETTER OF COMFORT A written instrument issued by A, where A agrees to make every effort to assure B's compliance with the terms of contract but without committing A to perform B's obligation in the event that B is unable to fulfil his obligation. Usually issued by a parent company on behalf of a subsidiary in another country.

LETTER OF CREDIT A letter empowering the bearer to obtain money from the party addressed. An LC is prepared by a bank, usually renewed every three months at an agreed upon rate. It is used in international trade to guarantee to the supplier payment for goods ordered. On many occasions it is also confirmed by the receiving bank, 'LC opened and confirmed'. The customer's account is debited with the amount and his bank then instructs its corresponding bank to make it available on demand wherever the customer wants the money. The bank will send a sample of the customer's signature.

LEVEL ANNUITY SYSTEM This entails equal aggregate payments of principal and interest (ie with principal repayments made in gradually ascending amounts).

LEVEL REPAYMENT Repayment scheme whereby repayments are at a fixed level, even though the interest rate may change.

LEVERAGE (ratio US), GEARING (ratio UK) Ratio of debt/liabilities to equity/assets. Includes *debt* and *debt-equity ratios.*

LEVERAGED (HIGHLY) Having a high debt-equity ratio.

LEVERAGED BUYOUT, LBO Purchase of a company by a small group of investors, often including management, mostly with borrowed funds. The debt is usually repaid from the company's cash flow or from sale of assets.

LEVERAGED STOCKHOLDER Major stockholder who, because of his holdings and earning power, can obtain benefits for the company.

LIABILITY Anything owing to somebody else. Companies' and most individuals' liabilities are the assets of banks (ie loans). Banks' liabilities are the deposits they take from their customers and the bonds and bills they issue. If a company's assets do not exceed its liabilities it is insolvent. The amount by which the one exceeds the other is the company's 'net worth'.

LIABILITY MANAGEMENT Supervision of the claims on the assets of a company.

LIBOR London Inter-Bank Offered Rate. The rate which top-class banks in London will pay each other for Eurodollars. Most Euro-market lending is pegged to three- or six-month LIBOR. The excess of the lending rate over LIBOR is the bank's margin (profit). LIBOR is a floating rate, changing all the time. Rates charged to Euro-market borrowers also change during the period of the loan. In America rates are pegged to the 'prime rate' as an alternative.

LIEN Obtaining of the rights to property (in the widest sense of the word) until a debt from the owner of the property is repaid. After a lien has been obtained, the debtor remains the legal owner of the property but he loses the right to sell it.

LIMITED LIABILITY It confines the losses that the owners of a company can incur to a maximum of the amount of capital that they have put in the company.

LIMITED RECOURSE FINANCE Finance arranged on the basis of the lender having recourse to the borrower only in certain circumstances (eg the loan to BP to finance the Forties oil field in the North Sea, where the lenders had no recourse to BP if there was insufficient oil).

LIMITATIONS (Statute of) If for six years no acknowledgment of a simple contract debt (as on an account or on a bill of exchange) has been made, the debtor may avoid payment of it by pleading this statute.

LIMIT ORDER Order to buy or sell a security at a specific price or better.

LINE OF CREDIT *See Backstop and Swingline.*

LIQUIDATION A company's final burial. The liquidator's main job is to get the maximum amount possible for the company's creditors from whatever assets are left.

LIQUIDITY *1* Short term assets like cash and easily sellable securities (as in liquidity ratio). From this can be deducted the short-term borrowing to get the net liquidity of a business.

2 The maturity of a financial market, ie the ability of investors to find buyers for their investments quickly and at the going market price.

LIQUIDITY PORTFOLIO Portfolio of assets in the form of cash or near-cash instruments.

LIQUIDITY PREMIUM A notional premium paid

by borrowers to lenders to encourage them to lend money at a fixed rate in the long term, when interest rates are likely to rise and it is therefore more profitable to invest in short-term paper.

LIQUID(ITY) RATIOS Current assets, less values of inventories, divided by current liabilities. Inventories are considered to be less readily realizable than other current assets which are regarded as 'liquid' assets. The ratio should be 1.0 or better. Ratios which reflect a borrower's ability to meet short-term obligations. They include the *acid-test* and the *current ratio*.

LISTED SECURITY An issue of a security accepted for trading on a stock exchange.

LISTING The process of public quotations on a stock exchange of a share or a bond.

LLCR Loan Life Cover Ratio. The loan must be recovered over the life period of the loan. During every year the proportionate part must be recovered.

LLRR Loan Life Recovery Ratio. The loan must be recovered over the whole life of the loan. During the first years there may be shortcomings but they must be recovered over the remaining years.

LOAN PORTFOLIO The unpaid loans of a lending organization.

LOAN STOCK The part of a company's capital issued in the form of interest-bearing long-term bonds or loans.

LOAN WITH EQUITY KICKER Loan at a reduced interest rate; when the proceeds from the project reach an agreed level, the loan converts into a quasi-equity loan, with the lender participating in the proceeds.

LOCK(ed) IN (interest rates) Refers to a fixed-interest loan with a long maturity so that the borrower is obliged to pay the fixed rate over a long period though other market rates may have fallen.

LOCK RATE Rate at which *drop lock* clause becomes operative.

LOMBARD RATE German term for the rate of interest charged for a loan against the security of pledged paper. Used with reference to the German Bundesbank, which usually keeps its Lombard rate about ½% above its discount rate.

LONDON INTERBANK OFFERED RATE, LIBOR The interest rate at which London banks are prepared to lend funds to first-class banks.

LONDON METAL EXCHANGE Housed in Plantation House in London City, where seven metals (copper, zinc, lead, tin, silver, aluminium and nickel) are traded by thirteen member dealers in the trading 'ring' (with a lot of screaming).

LONG TERM A loan with maturity exceeding five years. Bankers rarely lend for longer than fifteen years.

LONG TERM DEBT RATIO Ratio of long term debt to total assets.

LONGS British Government securities (gilts) with a maturity of more than fifteen years.

• •

MAG STRIPE The magnetic stripe on the back of a plastic credit card that allows electronic machinery to check that the card belongs to the person who uses it. In more modern cards an additional chip is inserted containing extra security elements.

MAIL TRANSFER Letter from a bank to its corresponding bank in another country authorizing payment to a named beneficiary in that country.

MAIN BANK Expression used to refer to the Japanese system of financing corporations. Every large corporation has one main bank which is closer to the company than any comparable relationship in Europe or America. The main bank has more information about the company than anybody else, lends more and monitors the company for all lenders.

MAKER Issuer of a debt instrument.

MANAGEMENT BUY-IN Similar to a 'buy-out' with the difference that the buyers of the company are a team of professional managers from outside the company rather than from within.

MANAGEMENT BUY-OUT, MBO Managers of a company become its owners by setting up a new company which buys the old company with money borrowed from banks. The assets of the company are used as collateral for the loan. Since this results invariably in the raising of the company's debt and reduces its equity, MBO's are often called leveraged buy-outs but leveraged buy-outs are not always done by the management.

MANAGEMENT COMMISSION *1* Fee charged by a bank for managing a credit or bond issue.
2 Fee charged for portfolio management.

MARGIN Deposit that an investor puts down to buy securities. The rest is often lent to him by his broker who is confident that the investor can always sell the security to repay the loan. The margin payment (the deposit) is designed to be at least as big as the maximum fluctuation possible in the market value of the security. If the price starts to fall dramatically the broker makes an extra 'margin-call' on the investor to increase his deposit.

MARGIN ACCOUNT Brokerage account allowing customers to buy securities with money borrowed from the broker.

MARGINAL RESERVE REQUIREMENT Additional deposits that by law depository institutions (banks) must set aside in their vaults or with the central bank.

MARKET CAPITALIZATION The total value of all of a firm's outstanding shares, calculated by multiplying the market price per share by the number of shares outstanding.

MARKET-CLEARING INTEREST RATE Interest rate which attracts equal number of buyers and sellers.

MARKET FAILURE The inability of the market to function in a normal manner.

MARKET INTERMEDIATION Acting on the market on behalf of someone else.

MARKETIZATION Increased reliance of banks on funds obtained either directly from financial markets or from clients but where the interest rates are set by reference to market-determined rates.

MARKET MAKING Maintain firm bid and offer prices for a security or currency on a continuous basis.

MARKET TO MARKET EXPOSURE Exposure in securities or other contracts, calculated at current market prices.

MARKET VALUE What someone is prepared to pay now to obtain something. Loans have a market value because banks can usually find someone to buy them at a price.

MATADOR BOND Bond issued on the Spanish market, denominated in currencies other than the peseta. Today expressed in Euros but the name remains.

MATCHING The process by which a bank chooses assets (loans) which match its liabilities (deposits) in terms of currency, maturity or geographical region.

No bank matches the two sides of its balance sheet perfectly. If it did, it would not make much of a profit. The bank's skill resides in getting the right degree of mismatching of assets and liabilities to maximize profits.

MATURE INVESTMENT Investment just at the beginning of the stage at which it will start to become profitable.

MATURITY MISMATCH Borrowings and loans with different maturities, ie borrowings made by a bank on the capital market to finance certain loans before the money from loans due is received.

MATURITY TRANSFORMATION Re-borrowing in order to extend the maturity of a loan.

MEDIUM TERM Loans with an original maturity between one and five years, shorter than long term and longer than short term.

MERRY-GO-ROUND EFFECT The circulation of money through various sources, ending up where it started.

MEZZANINE FINANCING Mix of financing instruments, including equity, subordinated debt, completion guarantees and bridge financing, the balance of which changes as the risk profile of a project changes, ie as a project moves beyond construction into operation.

MEZZANINE LEVEL In a venture capital operation, the stage of a company's development immediately before going public.

MINIMAX LOAN Floating rate loan where the loan is indexed but with a minimum and maximum (usually to LIBOR).

MINT The place where metal is turned into coins, usually under government guidance or ownership.

MITI Japan's Ministry of International Trade and Industry.

MIXED CREDITS Also known as *crédits mixtes*. A mixture of trade and aid finance whereby exports to developing countries from developed ones are given every financial assistance available. The aid portion should not be less than 20%.

MONETARY BASE The currency in circulation in a economy plus the commercial banks' reserves deposited with the central bank.

MONEY CENTRE BANKS Bank based in a large financial centre (London, New York).

MONEY MARKET Market for short term debt instruments, certificates of deposit, commercial paper, banker's acceptances, Treasury bills, discount notes.

MONEY MARKET RATE Rate of interest in the money market.

MORAL HAZARD The possibility of loss being caused by or aggravated by dishonesty or carelessness.

MORATORIUM Period agreed between a borrower and a lender in which repayments of principal are allowed to lapse. Banks do not like to give moratoria on interest payments.

MORTGAGE A conditional conveyance of a property as security for money lent, becoming void on performance of the condition.

MORTGAGE-BACKED SECURITY Security backed by mortgages, whereby investors receive payments out of the interest and principal on the underlying mortgages.

MORTGAGE BOND A long-term security secured by a lien on specific assets, normally fixed assets such as real estate.

MORTGAGEE The person to whom a property is mortgaged, one who lends money on mortgage. The lender.

MORTGAGOR The person who receives the money lent on mortgage. The borrower.

MOY Middle of the year (financial and business-planning).

MULTICURRENCY CLAUSE A clause in a loan agreement stating that more than one currency may be used in paying or redeeming the loan.

MULTIMATERAL NETTING Procedure whereby a company with multinational trade flows is able to balance its debits and credits between the subsidiaries and associates leaving only the balance to be settled, thereby reducing its need for foreign currency.

N/A No Account.

NARROW MARKET Market in which only a small supply is available of whatever the market sells.

NARROW MONEY Easily available money, cash, chequing accounts, very short term liquid funds.

NEAR-MONEY, QUASI MONEY Assets resembling strict money savings deposits, certificates of deposit.

NEGATIVE AMORTIZATION LOAN Instalment loan having the annuity principal as a basis for computation, the fixed periodic payments increasing from time to time, ie annually or bi-annually. Initial instalments are typically insufficient to meet the interest accruing on the loan principal and unpaid balances of interest are added to principal outstanding. As the periodic instalments increase in value they become sufficient to meet the interest due and commence reducing the principal outstanding.

NEGATIVE PLEDGE CLAUSE Clause in a loan agreement obligating the borrower not to grant security without equally securing the loan in question.

NEGATIVE TERM TRANSFORMATION Borrowing short term and lending long-term (opposite: transformation).

NEGOTIABLE INSTRUMENT Instrument where the title passes on delivery and endorsement, where the current holder can sue in his own name, where no notice of assignment need to be given to the person liable on the instrument and where a holder in due course takes, free from any defect, the title of his predecessors. Examples: Bill of lading, cheques, promissory notes.

NEGOTIABLE ORDER OF WITHDRAWAL, NOW Interest-bearing chequing account.

NET Opposite of *gross*. What's left after a number of deductions have been made.

NET BENEFIT INVESTMENT RATIO Ratio between the present worth of net benefits and present worth of an investment; alternatively, the sum of present worths after the incremental net benefit stream has become positive, divided by the sum of present worths in the earlier years of the project.

NET CASH REQUIREMENTS Gross disbursements plus outstanding debts due to mature less repayments and sales of loans, less net income adjusted for non-cash items, less the increase in usable capital.

NET OPERATING INCOME Total operating income less total operating expenses (including depreciation) but not interest.

NET RESULT Profit or loss. Takes into account

exceptional elements that are added to the current result.

NET WORTH Share capital + capital surplus + earned surplus. The value of a company calculated by subtracting its outstanding liabilities from the current value of total assets. If this is negative the company is insolvent. *See also Stockholders' equity.*

NEW MONEY In the field of debt restructuring, additional finance provided by lending institutions as opposed to rollover of existing finance.

NINJA-LOAN A loan whereby the abbreviation stands for No Income No Job no Assets.

NOMINEE Someone whose name is used in place of somebody else.

NONCALLABLE BOND Bond that cannot be recalled or redeemed prior to maturity.

NONPERFORMING ASSETS Assets with no financial return.

NON-PERFORMING LOANS Loans considered to be non-performing when no interest has been paid on them for at least ninety days. Then they have to be reported in the banks' accounts.

NON-RECOURSE FINANCE Loan where the lenders look solely to the cash flow generated by the project being financed for repayment. There is no recourse to the sponsor of the project, so that the lenders assume all the commercial and political risks of the project.

NON-VOTING SHARES Shares which give their owners no voting rights in the company's affairs.

NO-RETURN EQUITY Equity which brings in no returns but is still in existence.

NOSTRO ACCOUNT Expression used by bank A when talking at bank B to refer to bank A's account with bank B. Based on Latin *noster*, meaning ours, our account with you.

NOTE *1* Paper money. *2* A type of debt security as in *floating rate note* and *promissory note.*

NOT NEGOTIABLE Cannot be transferred to another with the same rights as belonging to the original holder. A crossed cheque with the words 'not negotiable' warns all holders that if there is any flaw in the title to it the rightful owner may recover payment from whoever obtains cash for it.

NOVATION Replacement of one debt for another or replacement of one debtor for another.

NOW Negotiable Order of Withdrawal. Account that can only be opened by individuals (not corporations) at banks in America.

NUMBERED ACCOUNT Swiss invention designed to give depositors ultimate secrecy. This means that only a small number of people in the bank know the name of the account holder.

ODD LOT A stock-market transaction in a smaller number of shares than the usual minimum amount required for trading (often 100 shares).

OFF-BALANCE SHEET ACTIVITIES, OBS Business that does not generally involve booking assets, ie letters of credit.

OFF-COVER When countries are not sufficiently creditworthy to pay for loans with which they have bought their imports, export credit agencies put them 'off-cover', ie they refuse to guarantee bank loans for financing exports to those countries. This leaves three options:

(1) A bank takes the risk
(2) The exporter himself takes the risk
(3) The business is called off.

OFFSHORE Refers to financial operations transacted outside the country in question.

OFFSHORE BANKING The part of a country's banking business that is denominated in foreign currencies and transacted between foreigners. It is also called that for transactions between foreigners and residents. London is the world's biggest offshore banking centre. New York is also important for international banking business but most of it cannot be described as offshore since it is denominated in dollars, New York's domestic currency.

OLD LADY OF THREADNEEDLE STREET Affectionate nickname for the Bank of England. The origin of the name is a cartoon depicting the Prime Minister of the time, William Pitt the Younger, trying to steal the bank's gold from a chest on top of which an old (traditionally built) lady is firmly sitting.

ONLENDING Equivalent to re-lending in connection with new money loans. The funds are recorded as a deposit in the central bank but the foreign bank and the contractual borrower (usually the central bank) agree that the loan proceeds will be made available to a third party within the country of the borrower.

OPEN ACCOUNT Trade finance that is not backed by 'bills of exchange'. Almost all trading within national boundaries is financed on open account. Open account leaves the vendor at risk since payment can be by cheque (that can bounce), banker's draft, mail transfer or telegraphic or electronic transfer. OK when the seller trusts the buyer.

OPEN CHEQUE A cheque that is not crossed. It can be exchanged in a bank for cash, thus being more attractive to thieves. The bank handing over cash for an open cheque cannot tell whether the recipient of the cash is the rightful owner.

OPEN END INVESTMENT FUND Fund that is open in the sense that it issues new shares every time it receives new money from investors, unlike a *closed-end investment fund* that issues only a limited number of shares that are traded only in a secondary market, in Britain called *unit trusts*.

OPENING PRICE Initial price at which a transaction in a security takes place on a given day.

OPEN-MARKET OPERATIONS Dealings by a central bank in the money market or securities in order to adjust the amount of money and credit floating around in an economy. When the central bank buys securities it pays for them with a cheque. The receiver puts it into his bank account, thereby increasing the total assets of the bank. When the central bank sells securities it is paid by a cheque coming out of the banking system. The cheque then disappears into the central bank's coffers and the 'money supply' is reduced.

OPEN PRICING Procedure whereby a bond issue is sold on the basis of a yield to be determined after the selling period is over.

OPERATING RATIO Ratio of operating costs (including depreciation) to total revenue. Total operating expenses, including depreciation (but excluding interest) divided by total operating revenue. The ratio should be 1.0 or under.

OPPORTUNITY COST What an investor loses by not putting his money into an investment that would earn him a return.

OPTION A contract giving the holder the right to buy or sell an underlying security, commodity or currency before a certain date.

OUTPUT GAP The difference between an

economy's actual GDP and its potential GDP: a level of output consistent with full employment and historical trends in productivity.

OUTWARD SWAP Spot purchase of foreign exchange and forward resale of the same currency against domestic currency.

OUTWARD SWITCHING OPERATIONS Movement of domestic currency assets into foreign currency.

OVERAGE LOAN Special loan issued to cover excess costs on a project.

OVERDRAFT A banking practice of giving borrowers a credit facility and letting them draw on it as they will. Overdrafts are popular with companies or individuals for their flexibility. The cost price of an overdraft is much higher than the normal interest rate on loans.

OVERNIGHT FUNDS Short-term funds borrowed to be returned by the following business day.

OVER-THE-COUNTER MARKET Market for securities not listed in any of the exchanges (about 80% of total securities in the US). Includes US Government and agency issues, state and local government bonds and shares, many public utility bonds and shares, and most corporation and bank shares.

P

PACKAGE LOAN (IFC) A loan administered by a national development bank on behalf of IFC. The development bank subdivides the loan into smaller loans which it lends to small and medium size enterprises.

PAID-UP CAPITAL The amount paid by shareholders for a company's issued shares. Some shares may have been issued in partly paid form in which case the paid-up capital will be less than the issued capital. Further calls may then be made on shareholders to fork out the rest at a later date.

PAID-UP STOCK, FULLY PAID STOCK Stock fully paid for (ie upon which no further subscription instalments are due).

PAR, PAR VALUE, FACE VALUE The principal or

nominal value appearing on a bond, note, coupon, piece of money or other instrument. Shares are sold at 'face value' as opposed to being sold at a discount to their face value. Equality of nominal and market value; 'above par' means at a premium; 'below par' at a discount. 'Mint Par' is the nominal par of exchange in foreign exchange and is the rate at which the standard coin of one country is convertible into that of another. When the gold standard was still applicable it showed the quantity of gold as compared with the gold sovereign, ie value in pure gold between gold standard countries.

PARALLEL FINANCING Co-financing but with the partners financing different parts of the project.

PARENT BANK Bank in a major industrial country that sets up a subsidiary in a developing country.

PARI PASSU CLAUSE Clause in loan agreement precluding subordination of a loan to other debt. In the issue of new shares, it states that the new shares will rank equally for dividend with an existing similar issue.

PARIS CLUB Informal group of creditor governments who meet in Paris (usually at the offices of the World Bank, Avenue d'Iéna) to discuss and eventually reschedule loans that some developing countries have not been able to repay. The loans include government-to- government credits and officially guaranteed export credits. In the London Club private creditors meet.

PARTICIPATION Joining in new issues of securities of new loans by banks at a lower level, ie after all the big fee-earning jobs in underwriting or syndicating have been distributed.

PARTICIPATION CERTIFICATE Security incorporating the right to participate in the ownership of a corporation but without some of the rights granted to shareholders, such as the right to vote at shareholders' meetings.

PARTICIPATION FEE A fee given to a bank participating in a Euro-loan.

PARTNERSHIP SHARE A share in a partnership.

PASS-THROUGH CERTIFICATE, or **PARTICIPATION CERTIFICATE** Certificate representing an interest in a pool of funds.

PASS-THROUGHS, PASS-THROUGH SECURITIES Securities representing pooled debt obligations repackaged as shares, that passes income from debtors through the intermediary investors.

The most common type is a mortgage-backed certificate.

PAYEE One to whom a bill of exchange, promissory note or cheque is made payable.

PAYING AGENT In the issue of international securities, a firm (usually a bank) responsible for arranging for the payment of cash or cheques to holders of the securities who will be receiving interest or dividend.

PAYMENT PERIOD Interval between semi-annual dates on which repayment on IBRD loans is due.

PAYOUT DATE, PAYMENT DATE, DISTRIBUTION DATE Date on which a due periodic payment is made, as for bonds or stock dividend.

PAYOUT PRICE Difference between the face value of a bond and the net value received by the bondholder, after deducting commission or taxes.

PAWNBROKER He lends money on the security of property deposited with him. The loan is always much lower than the value of the property. If borrowers repay the money and the interest due within six months they can get their property back. If they do not repay, the pawnbroker has the right to sell the goods. In England these shops could be recognized by the sign of three golden balls hanging outside.

P/E RATIO Price/earnings ratio. Market price per ordinary share divided by earnings per ordinary share after tax. It expresses the market value placed on the expectation of future earnings.

PERFORMANCE BOND Guarantee from a bank to an importer (often provided by the exporter's bank) that the exporter will fulfil his contract in accordance with stipulated terms and conditions. Often used in the construction industry when the buyer wants some hold over the construction company to ensure that it completes a project on time and as promised. The builder pays a periodic premium to the banker (per trimester, yearly, etc)

PERIODIC REVIEW CLAUSE, REVIEW CLAUSE A clause in a loan agreement, particularly policy based lending, which gives the lender the right to determine periodically whether the stated objectives are being met and whether any problems have been encountered. If problems occur, further disbursement can be withheld.

PERPETUAL BOND Non-maturing, non-redeemable government bond.

PERPETUAL FLOATING RATE NOTE A floating rate note with interest paid on a three monthly basis but which is renewable every six months. (It has a floating maturity.)

PER PROCURATIONEM (pp or per pro) Signed by an authorized person on behalf of his principal.

PERSONAL LOAN Bank loan to an individual in which the interest and principal are bundled together and repaid in monthly instalments over an agreed upon period. Usually the rates are very expensive.

PERSONAL STOCK Registered stock.

PIGGYBACK FINANCING Financing studies for a future project as part of a loan to finance another project usually in the same sector.

PINK SHEET Sheets printed in the USA on pink paper. They list all brokers who deal in markets in over-the-counter-stocks and American depositary receipts.

PIPELINE FACTOR The ratio of appraisal departures to the number of operations required to complete a World Bank (IBRD) lending programme (for loans that have passed the preparation stage).

PIT The part of the trading floor where futures contracts are bought and sold by much hand waving and shouting. Despite the name, the 'pits' are raised, not sunk.

PLACEMENT MEMORANDUM A document prepared by the lead manager of a syndicate in the Euro-credit market which seeks to give sufficient information to other potential lenders to enable them to decide on participation.

PLAIN VANILLA SWAP, VANILLA SWAP, CLASSIC SWAP A five to seven-year swap of six month LIBOR-based floating rate funds against fixed rate funds, both denominated in US dollars.

POISON PILL A defensive action by a company that fears being taken over. Poison pills are financial schemes or changes in the articles of agreement that are triggered by a takeover and put the company in trouble.

POLICY BASED LENDING Loans made in support of policy and institutional changes, rather than for specific projects. Normally given under the structural adjustment and sector adjustment lending programmes.

POLICY FRAMEWORK PAPER, PFP Vehicles for country authorities to reach agreement with the World Bank or the International Monetary Fund on the broad outline of medium-term programmes to overcome balance of payment problems and foster growth. In their final form they are statements of governments of their objectives and policies over a rolling three-year period with annual updates and revisions.

POOL-BASED LENDING RATE SYSTEM
Lending based on the pool-based variable lending rate. The lending is adjusted every six months to achieve a given spread above the average cost of outstanding borrowings (IBRD).

POOLED LOAN A loan included in the currency pooling system.

PORTFOLIO A collection of financial assets belonging to a single owner. The more the portfolio is diversified the lower the risk.

PORTFOLIO MANAGER Person responsible for supervizing an investment portfolio.

POST (A RATE) Set a rate for a financial instrument.

POST-DATED CHEQUE Cheque with a future date written on. The payee cannot get the cheque paid to him until the future date. Before then the payer can always cancel the cheque.

PRAECIPIUM The amount the lead manager of a Euro-credit takes for his own fee before dividing the remainder of the management fee among the rest of the management group.

PRE-EMPTIVE BID A bid for a company that is set at a high price with the aim of discouraging any other counter-bidders.

PREFERENCE SHARES These shares give their owner a fixed dividend, as opposed to ordinary shares where dividend depends on the profits of the company. These shareholders have a right to their dividend before any payment made to other shareholders. If a company goes bust, preference shareholders are entitled to a maximum of the nominal value of whatever assets are left. Ordinary shareholders get whatever is left after that.

PREFERENTIAL CREDITOR A creditor of a company who, in case of bankruptcy, has preferential claim on whatever assets are left over and above the claims of ordinary creditors.

PREFERRED STOCK Stock which has a claim upon the earnings (and sometimes upon the assets and control) of a corporation prior to the common or other class stock.

PREMATURED LOAN Loan that matures before time initially specified.

PREMIUM Foreign exchange: opposite of discount. Option market: price at which an option sells. Securities: the difference between the par value and the higher market value of a security expressed as a percentage of the par value. Stocks: difference between the par value and the selling price of the share when the selling price is higher. Swap: a swap with an above market rate.

PREPAYMENT FEE Fee payable for a loan redeemed before maturity.

PRICE Price includes face value, interest and any premium or discount.

PRICE-EARNINGS RATIO Is supposed to be the ultimate test if a company's shares are undervalued. It is the ratio of a company's stock-market value to its latest annual earnings after tax profit. In other words it is the number of years it would take an investor to get his money back if the company kept its profits constant and distributed all of them every year, but companies do none of that.

PRIMARY DEALER One of the major banks and investment dealers in the US authorized to buy and sell government securities in direct dealing with the Federal Reserve.

PRIMARY MARKET Market for new securities. Contrasts with 'secondary market'.

PRIME BORROWER, PREMIER BORROWER, HIGH QUALITY BORROWER, TOP GRADE BORROWER The most creditworthy type of borrower.

PRIME RATE In the USA: the rate charged by banks to preferential customers (*taux de base*).

PRINCIPAL Face value of the loan. To be distinguished from 'interest' which is what is to be paid every year for the principal. In mortgage loans you will notice that interest is at the beginning always higher than the part of principal.

PRIVATE BANK Bank owned by a limited number of partners, each of whom bears unlimited liability for the debts of the bank. Since they do not have to report publicly too many details of their business, private banks are popular in secretive Switzerland.

PRIVATE PAPER Paper placed with a limited group of investors and not advertized.

PRIVATE PLACING The sale of a large part of a new issue to a small group of investors. Usually big institutions like insurance companies and pension funds.

PRIVATIZATION The sale to the private sector of business that has been run by the government, sometimes after it had been 'nationalized', ie private business taken over by government. It can be done by the government to earn cash or because government made a mess of it.

PROCESSING FEE Fee which the World Bank has considered levying on the full amount of loan commitments. Same as 'front-end-fee'.

PRODUCTION-SHARING CONTRACT Contract where the contractor makes contributions to the investment project and his remuneration depends mainly (not necessarily wholly) on a share of the production of the investment project, including the right to purchase such share at a predetermined price or at a price determined under an agreed formula.

PROFITABILITY RATIO, REVENUE COVENANT RATIO Ratio that measures the return on assets.

PROFIT-SHARING CONTRACT Contract where the contractor makes contributions to the investment project and his remuneration substantially depends on the revenues or profits of the project.

PRO-FORMA INVOICE A first step of getting an export order, the first draft of an exporter's bill to an importer. The invoice contains estimated prices on the basis of which the importer decides whether to place the order or not.

PROGRAMME ADJUSTMENT LOAN, PAL (IBRD) Loan to assist a country to make adjustments to a series of relatively short-term economic policy objectives.

PROGRAMME LOAN (IBRD) Bank loan given not for a specific project but to help a country overcome unforeseen temporary difficulties which would otherwise result in inappropriate long-term policy adjustments to correct short-term balance-of-payment problems.

PROJECT FINANCING Financing wherein the lender looks to a project's cash flows to repay the principal and interest on debt and to a project's assets for security; also known as 'structured financing' because it requires structuring of debt and equity so that a project's cash flows are adequate to service the debt. Used mainly for big projects such as mining, ports.

PROJECT NOTE Short-term paper issued by

municipalities to finance short-term cash flows for a specific project.

PROJECT PREPARATION FACILITY, PPF (IBRD or IDA) *See also piggyback financing* – providing funds for small tasks. As an advance to prepare a project repaid through reimbursement under the loan/credit for the project itself.

PROMISSORY NOTE An unconditional promise in writing made by one person to another signed by the maker, engaging to pay, on demand or at a fixed or determinable future time, a sum of money to or to the order of a specified person or to bearer.

PROSPECTUS A document prepared by the lead manager containing all the pertinent information about a public offering of securities and about the borrower. It is made available to the appropriate legal authorities, stock exchanges and the prospective investors. Also called 'offering memorandum'.

PROTECTIONISM Used to refer to any barriers to trade of which the users disapproved. Protectionism was mainly responsible for the decline in world trade in the period 1929 to 1932 that nearly caused the collapse of the international financial system. Also in the 1980s there was quite a lot of it. Developing countries are still finding stiff barriers for their exports to Western countries. There is the dualism of rich countries complaining of dumping prices from developing countries whilst they in reality fear destruction of their own domestic industries. On the other hand when developing countries cannot export they do not earn enough to reimburse their loans. This is mainly the case for agricultural products whereby the agri-lobby is very powerful in rich countries.

PROTEST OF A BILL OF EXCHANGE A written declaration by a notary public that the bill has been duly presented and payment in acceptance refused.

PROVISIONS Money set aside by banks, out of earnings, against a rainy day. Mostly provisions are calculated as a percentage of a bank's loans to doubtful debtors. There are 'specific' provisions against specifically identifiable debtors that look bad. 'General' provisions are not linked to specific borrowers but based on expected market conditions that can have an effect on borrowers that are not yet identified as 'doubtful'.

PROXY FIGHT A technique for gaining control of

a company or to induce it to make major changes without actually paying for it. A small group of shareholders tries to convince the rest to enable the group either to make the change or to change the board or allow some of its members onto the board.

PROXY VOTE The way to influence a company's meeting without being there. A proxy vote is delegated to somebody else by the person who actually has the voting power. Used often by shareholders who cannot attend an annual or an extraordinary general meeting.

PRUDENTIAL RATIOS Ratios that regulators consider to be prudent for banks to maintain between different items on their balance sheets (for instance capital ratio, liquidity ratio). In some countries these ratios are strictly laid down in statutes; in others they are more flexible to be interpreted by bank supervisor organizations.

PUBLIC COMPANY A company that offers its shares to the general public, as opposed to a private company owned by a small group. A private company can go 'public' by a new issue of shares. When its shares then get recognized on a stock exchange, it becomes a 'quoted company'.

PUBLIC ENTERPRISE REFORM LOAN World Bank loan to help reform the finances of a public enterprise.

PUBLIC OFFERING The offering of an original issue of stock through public sale.

PUT A right to redeem a debt instrument before maturity at par under specific circumstances outlined in the original agreement.

• •

QUALITY LOAN A bank loan which has been carefully prepared and is financially viable.

QUASI-EQUITY, QUASI-CAPITAL Includes equity-like instruments and other forms of loans that have the form of equity or equity that has the form of a loan. Example: equity with a put agreement, ie unlike normal equity, the investor requires return of the equity in, for example, five years at 10% interest.

QUEUE Waiting list for the issue of securities.

QUICK RATIO *See acid-test ratio.*

QUOTED COMPANY Company whose shares are quoted on a recognized stock exchange. To obtain this the company must meet certain standards foreseen by the exchange. After that it will have to maintain prescribed levels of disclosure. In return, the exchange makes the company's shares marketable by providing a price and place where buyers and sellers meet.

R

● ●

RATE The price of money, either to borrow it (interest rate) or to exchange it for someone else's money (exchange rate).

RATING Evaluation of a corporation or a security, particularly as regards the solvability of the corporation. Standard & Poor's, Moody's and Fitch's are the best known rating agencies in the USA, in France the *Agence française d'évaluation financière (ADEF).* Standard & Poor's and Fitch's ratings for bonds range from AAA, AA and A for the highest quality to DDD, DD and D for the lowest quality. Moody's ranges from AAA, AA and A to CCC,CC and C and MIG1 to MIG4 for short-term municipal notes. ADEF ranges from AAA, AA and A to D for bonds and T1 to T4 for commercial paper.

RATIONAL EXPECTATIONS A theory based, first on the assumption that individuals and companies will try to maximize their own welfare, that is they will try to make their own economic and other circumstances as desirable as possible, and second, that, as individuals and companies make economic decisions in their own interest, they do so in such a way that markets move towards equilibrium, easing inflation.

RD Refer to drawer of cheque.

REAL ESTATE INVESTMENT TRUST, REIT Organization which collects funds from individuals for reinvestment in property. The funds are normally collected by the sale of shares of ownership in the trust.

REAL INTEREST RATE Normal rate less rate of inflation, divided by one plus the rate of inflation.

REAL RATE OF RETURN The difference between the actual rate of return from an investment and a specified measure of the rate of inflation. It can be positive or negative.

RECALL With loans made prior to the introduction of the currency pool, each loan was disbursed in the currencies available at that time. As regards repayment of the loan, the World Bank determines the order in which currencies shall be repaid (usually according to which currency has the most attractive investment potential). The choice of currency by the WB for repayment purposes is called recall.

RECAPITALIZATION Altering the capital structure of a corporation by increasing or decreasing its capital stock.

RECAPTURE CLAUSE Clause in a loan agreement that allows a lender to recover part or all of his previously lent assets if economic circumstances improve.

RECEIVABLES Money owed to a company and not yet received. This is watched attentively by banks. When this figure goes up too fast a company may not be able to pay its own debt and go bankrupt even if it is making a balance sheet profit. Usually it is expressed in number of days.

RECEIVER A financial technician (accountant or solicitor) called in by a troubled company's creditors to sort out its financial problems.

RECIPROCITY Theory, favoured in the USA, to allow a foreign bank or company to do as much business as it is allowed to do in the foreign country. Of course not all countries have equal levels of trade resulting in reactions by the smaller volume country to disagree with reciprocity.

RECOGNIZED BANK The Bank of England allows 'recognized banks' and 'licensed deposit-taking institutions'. Recognized banks can carry out a wider range of banking business but, in return, they have to provide greater insurances of their expertise and standing.

RECONCILIATION The process of controlling a company's own record of financial transactions with that of its bankers allowing for un-cleared cheques that are yet to be paid in or out.

RED CLAUSE In a documentary credit, special clause included which allows the seller to obtain an advance from the correspondent bank to finance the manufacture or purchase of goods to be delivered under the documentary credit. Liability is assumed by the issuing bank rather than by the corresponding bank. It is called a *red clause* because red ink is used to draw attention to the clause.

REDEMPTION The exchange of securities for cash or for other securities at the time they mature ('on redemption'). Securities are redeemable 'at par'.

RED HERRING Preliminary prospectus issued to obtain an indication of interest in the issue. It is incomplete because it does not contain the public offering price, the underwriter's discount or the date of issue.

REDISCOUNT Resale of instruments such as banker's acceptances already discounted by lender, usually with central bank or discount house, at a price less than the face value.

REFERENCE BANK A bank with interest rates used as a base for determining the rates of a loan or other form of credit.

REFINANCING Paying off existing debt with new (and cheaper) loans. If this is tried when interest rates are falling banks will impose penalty clauses for early repayment of debt but it may still be a profitable exercise. 'Refinancing' is smart but calling it 'rescheduling' is not.

REFINANCING RISK Risk of being able to refinance short-term borrowings under suitable conditions when these borrowings mature.

REFUNDING Replacing (usually by governments) one issue of debt with another at the moment one comes to maturity.

REGISTERED SECURITY A security where ownership is determined by the name in which it is registered as opposed to a bearer security where ownership is determined by who possesses it.

REGISTERED STOCK, PERSONAL STOCK Stock which cannot be transferred without placing the signature of the owner upon the books of the issuing corporation and delivery of the certificate.

REGULAR LENDING PROGRAMME The World Bank lending programme that includes the base lending programme and the standby programme.

REGULATION Binding laws of the EC. They prescribe the time limits within which member states must introduce Community rules into their own domestic legislation.

REISSUE Issue placed into circulation again after a specific lapse of time.

RELENDING An operation whereby, when a domestic debtor repays a foreign debt, the funds are relent by the foreign creditor to a second debtor within the same country.

REMITTANCE Money sent from one country to another, often by migrant workers sending money home to their families in their country of origin. In some countries this a major source of foreign income.

RENEWAL The act or process of transforming or extending a credit agreement, whereby the old debt is cancelled by the establishment of a new one.

REPOS Short for sale and repurchase agreements. Repos are contracts between a broker and a bank or company with some surplus cash. The bank, which can be the Federal Reserve bank, buys the securities and agrees to sell them back at a future date (a few days hence) at an agreed price. During this period the broker may have found a long-term investor who agrees to buy them.

REPURCHASE AGREEMENT Arrangement by banks and other institutions to borrow short-term (usually one day) money by transferring securities to the lender, with the agreement that they will buy them back.

RESCHEDULING Putting off till later what you cannot pay today. Found often in developing countries.

RESERVE BANK *See Central Bank Facility.*

RESERVE RATIO The fraction of demand deposit money which a commercial bank must keep in its reserve account. This ratio determines the maximum amount of money a bank may lend out. In the USA the legal reserve requirement is imposed by the Federal Reserve on depository institutions. The reserves (cash maintained in a bank's own vault or claims on cash on deposit with compulsory or optional depositories) for transaction accounts are 3% on $25 million or less and 12% for larger sums. In France the ratio was 60% with reserves being defined as *disponibilités... realisations des actifs de négociation facile figurant au bilan*. The new system has been in place since September 1988, with the ratio being set at 100%.

RESERVES What a company keeps 'in reserve'. They are mostly retained profits, profits that are not paid out as dividends to shareholders. Technically they belong to the shareholders but they can be kept as a buffer for a large expenditure.

RESETTER LOAN, RATE RESETTER LOAN
Loan where the interest rate is fixed for a specific period and reset after a specific period of time.

RESOURCE MOBILIZATION RATIO The ratio between available resources and use of those resources.

RETAIL BANKING Traditional banking operations conducted with the general public.

RETAIL INVESTOR Investor who buys securities and commodities futures on his own behalf, not for an organization.

RETAINED EARNINGS Accumulated net income, less distribution to stockholders and transfers to paid-in capital accounts.

RETIRED DEBT A debt that has been paid off.

RETOUR SANS PROTE(S)T Endorsed on a bill of exchange indicates that the endorser does not want any expense to be incurred if there is any irregularity.

RETRACTABLE, PUTABLE BOND Bond where a coupon is determined for a limited number of years, after which a new coupon is determined, with bondholders at the same time having the right to early redemption.

RETURN ON ASSETS, ROA Net income divided by average earning assets (loans and investment).

RETURN ON AVERAGE ASSETS Net income as a percentage of total disbursed loan and equity investments net of reserves and liquid assets averaged for the current period and previous fiscal year.

RETURN ON AVERAGE NET WORTH Net income as a percentage of the paid-in share capital and accumulated earnings averaged for the current period and previous fiscal year.

RETURNS Cheques which for one reason or another are sent back to the branch bank at which they were originally presented. The reason may be that they were incorrectly filled in.

REVENUE-ANTICIPATION NOTE Short-term municipal borrowings that fund current operations and are funded by revenues other than taxes, especially US federal aid.

REVENUE BOND Long-term borrowings that are used to fund specific projects. They are repaid from the income that will be generated by the project.

REVERSE PURCHASE AGREEMENT
Repurchase agreement initiated by the lender of funds.

REVERSE SWAP A swap which offsets the interest rate or currency exposure on an existing swap. It can be written with the original counter-party or with a new counter-party. In either case, it is typically executed to realize capital gains.

REVOLVING CREDIT, ROLLOVER CREDIT A line of credit that can be borrowed against up to a stated credit limit and into which repayments go for crediting. A loan in which, as soon as part has been repaid, can immediately be borrowed again. It has an upper limit that can be borrowed and no limit on the number of times that limit amount can be reached on condition that it had been repaid before.

REVOLVING FUND A fund for project-related expenditure.

RIGHT Usually in connection with new share issues. It gives the investor the right to purchase further shares at a given price.

RIGHTS ISSUE A new issue of securities offered first to existing holders of the company's securities at a discount to the market price.

RING Part of the London Metal Exchange where trading takes place.

RISK The danger inherent in borrowing money from one person and lending it to another. Different ways in which deposits can be mutated into loans give rise to different risks: exchange risk: taking dollar deposits and making sterling loans; interest rate risk: taking deposits linked to LIBOR and making fixed-rate loans; maturity risk: taking deposits with a short number of days' notice of withdrawal and making loans repayable for a year; political risk: collecting dollars in the USA and lending to Argentina; credit risk: taking money from a reputable firm and lending to a doubtful character.

RISK-AVERSE The extent to which an investor is reluctant to take a risk.

RISK CAPITAL Capital invested in high-risk or relatively high-risk securities and enterprises, in expectation of very high returns. It is sometimes used of equities or ordinary stock, the dividend of which varies with the profits earned by the corporation.

RISK PREMIUM The extra yield over the risk-free

rate owing to various types of risk inherent to a particular investment.

ROLLING GUARANTEE A guarantee that would cover, at any time, only one or two payment installments but would, if the covered payments are met, 'roll' to subsequent payments.

ROLLOVER 1 Reinvestment of money received from a maturing security in a similar security.
2 Term used for a delay allowed by a lender to a borrower in making a principal payment on a loan. With governments, rollovers in the form of re-fundings or re-financings are routine.

ROLLOVER DATE Date of adjustment of interest rate in maturity transformation.

ROLLOVER OF GAINS Reinvestment of profits.

ROLY POLY BOND Medium- or long-term bond where annual coupon is renewed every three years, at which time the investor may be reimbursed.

ROUND-TRIPPING Situation whereby foreign currency denominated debt is purchased at a discount and redeemed for full face value in the local currency, thereby encouraging capital flight.

RUF Revolving Underwriting Facility.

RUN 'A run on the bank': when depositors run to their nearest bank branch to get their money out as fast as possible when they fear that the bank will default.

RUNNING (WEIGHTED) AVERAGE The average rate of interest applied to an outstanding loan, based on the rates applied on all previous disbursements, weighted, where necessary, to allow for different levels of disbursement.

S

SALES AGENT, SELLING AGENT Firm or individual carrying out a sale of securities.

SAMURAI BOND Bond issued on the Japanese market in yen outside Japan.

SARAKIN Unregulated Japanese hire-purchase outfits also referred to as loan sharks. Japan's domestic interest rates are strictly controlled and credit is not allocated by price but by government edict. Industry gets first priority but consumers do not get credit so easily. That is when the sarakin get into the picture at highly inflated rates (up to 100%).

SAVINGS BANK In older days, banks that accepted only deposits of small savers, did no business with industry and provided no money-transmission service. Today, savings banks are becoming all-in-one banks, lend to industry, give personal loans, provide cheque books and credit cards etc.

SAVINGS BOND (France, Belgium, USA) Short- or medium-term fixed interest bearer bond issued by a public credit institution or commercial bank. It is not marketable. *Bons de caisse* are general French savings bonds. *Bons d'épargne* are five year savings bonds issued at par. The bearer can ask to be reimbursed after three months but the amount he is paid increases over the five year period.

SCHEDULED DEBT SERVICE Debt service that follows a set schedule.

SCORING Technique for evaluating a borrower, primarily his ability to repay a loan.

SCRIP CERTIFICATE, BEARER SCRIP Written obligation of a bank acting as paying agent for an issue, to hand over to the subscriber the definite certificates as soon as they have been issued.

SCRIP ISSUE, STOCK DIVIDEND The issue of additional stock free of charge to stockholders in proportion to the stock they already hold.

SEASONED ISSUE Issue of securities that have gained a reputation in the market for reliability.

SEC Securities and Exchange Commission. American federal agency set up to oversee the securities industry. It has 5 commissioners and 2000 staff. Based in Washington DC. Its main weapon to keep the markets clean is disclosure. Issuers of securities in America have to reveal far more about themselves than securities in other countries.

SECONDARY MARKET Market for transactions in existing securities. In France: *second marché*. In UK: *unlisted securities*. In USA: *over-the-counter market* or *third market*.

SECOND TIER BANK *1* Bank used as secondary source of funds.

2 Smaller lenders, banks other than the main commercial banks (mainly in Latin America).

SECTOR ADJUSTMENT LOAN Loan aiming at major policy improvements in a sector.

SECURED LOAN A loan that provides a lender with the right to take over certain prescribed assets of the borrower should the borrower fail to repay. These assets may be physical (property or goods) or they may be only documents entitling the holder to certain payments.

SECURITIES Documents (shares, bonds) which give the holder title to the investment.

SECURITIES ANALYST Person carrying out systematic assessment of securities as a basis for investment strategy.

SECURITIES DEALER, SECURITIES FIRM Firm acting as a principal rather than an agent in the securities market.

SECURITIES MARKET The primary and secondary market for negotiable equity (stocks) and long-term debt instruments (bonds).

SECURITIZATION *1* Issue of securities in exchange for debt. The World Bank calls it 'the packaging and selling of a pool of creditor risks in the form of a security'. In French: *titrisation*.
2 The tendency of financial markets to make greater use of securities. Firms issue securities rather than borrow from banks.

SECURITY *1* Document giving title to property or claim on income.
2 Income-yielding paper traded on the stock exchange or secondary market.

SEGMENT, SECTOR (of the market) A particular part of the market, eg airline stocks. Securities analysts often specialize in one segment of the market.

SELF-LIQUIDATING CREDIT Credit reimbursed by the income from operation for which it is lent.

SELL-DOWN The transfer of a credit from a bank within the syndicate to a bank outside the syndicate.

SENIOR DEBT Debt for which claims on assets of the borrower rank ahead of other debts in case of liquidation.

SENIORITY The order of priority for repayment of debt.

SERIAL BOND, LOAN *1* Bond issues split into a series of maturities.
2 Special type of serial bonds where reimbursements decided by drawing in lots.

SERVICE A LOAN Pay interest due on a loan.

SET ASIDE AGREEMENT Agreement for payment of receipts from a project to be designated for a specific purpose.

SETTLEMENT DATE Date on which payment for a transaction must be made.

SHADOW PRICE *See Accounting price.*

SHAKE-OUT (of the market) *1* A moderate stock market or business recession, usually corrective of an inflationary condition.
2 Any movement in the market prices or securities that forces speculators to sell their holdings.

SHARE LIST A listing of stocks with their current prices.

SHARE OWNERSHIP The possession of shares of stock in a corporation.

SHARING CLAUSE, PAYMENT SHARING CLAUSE Clause in a loan agreement where, if one of the participants fails to receive payment, the others will share receipts with the participant(s) not receiving payment.

SHELF REGISTRATION A system of standing authorization to issue securities given by the US treasury to certain select borrowers (including the IBRD). Borrowers must normally wait for formal approval.

SHOGUN BOND Non-resident bond issues denominated in foreign currencies on the Tokyo market.

SHORT BILLS Bills drawn for any period within ten days of their maturity.

SHORT HEDGE Hedging operation by someone who is 'short' (who owns less of an item than he has contracts to deliver).

SHORT LEASH APPROACH Approach to debt restructuring whereby the restructuring agreement only applies for a short period of time.

SHORT POSITION Where a dealer in stocks or commodities is committed to sell more of them than he has available for sale.

SHORT SALE Sale by dealers of securities they do not own.

SHORT-TERM NOTE Note with maturity of one year or less.

SIGHT DEPOSIT Money that can be withdrawn from a bank almost immediately like current accounts deposits, overnight deposits from other banks and money lent 'at call'.

SIGHT DRAFT Draft payable on demand, to be distinguished from *usuance draft* which is payable at some future date.

SINKING FUND A fund created by a borrower for the purpose of redeeming bonds. The borrower is obliged to redeem specified amounts of the bond within the specified periods.

SOFT LOAN Money lent on soft terms, ie more generous than those available in the market. Loans from the International Development Association, part of the World Bank, are called soft because they give loans for periods up to 50 years with 0% interest, 0.75% of administrative cost and 1% on the not yet disbursed amount. These loans give grace periods of five to ten years. The result is that only about 8 cents to the dollar is to be reimbursed.

SOGO BANK Regional finance institutions in Japan, dealing mainly with smaller enterprises.

SOLVENCY The state of having assets worth more than the liabilities, opposite is 'insolvency'. This is not to be confused with 'liquidity'. One is not liquid when unable to pay one's debt on time. An illiquid company can become insolvent.

SOLVENCY RATIO The ratio between capital and assets. *See also Capital ratio.*

SOUTH SEA BUBBLE A share where the price gets kicked up higher and higher until people realize that it is little more than hot air. The origin was the South Sea Company established in 1710 and given a monopoly on trading in the south Pacific. It became so powerful that its was allowed to buy up the national debt before investors lost confidence and the bubble burst.

SOVEREIGN A British gold coin representing £1 sterling but worth much more. It is a standard 7.998 grams (0.25 troy ounces) in weight. The coins are sometimes called 'kings' and 'queens' depending on the sovereign whose head is portrayed on the coin.

SOVEREIGN CREDIT A borrowing guaranteed by the state.

SOVEREIGN RISK The risk of changes in a borrowing country's overall foreign exchange position, which might affect its ability to repay a loan.

SOVEREIGN RISK LOAN Loan to a state or loan where the state takes the responsibility for the loan.

SPECIAL COMMITMENT (IBRD) Bank procedure whereby the WB provides a commercial bank with a guarantee to enable it to issue a letter of credit to a bank borrower to finance the purchase of goods under a project.

SPECIAL PLACEMENT Placement issued by

international development institutions and placed directly with central banks, monetary authorities and governments.

SPECULATIVE GRADE PAPER Issue of paper rated BB+ or below by a rating company.

SPINOFF The transfer by a corporation of a portion of its assets to a newly formed corporation in exchange for the latter's capital stock, which is thereupon distributed as a dividend to the stockholders of the first corporation.

SPLIT, SPLIT-UP, SPLITTING Increasing the number of shares of a corporation by ratio or multiple.

SPOT CREDIT Short-term credit where the amount and conditions are negotiated as required.

SPOT MARKET, ACTUAL MARKET, CASH MARKET, PHYSICAL MARKET Market where goods are sold for cash, for immediate delivery.

SPOT PRICE The buying or selling quoted for a transaction to be made on the spot, usually referring to transactions in the foreign exchange markets. Spot prices contrast with prices for futures and options contracts.

SPREAD *1* Options: Purchase of a call option at one price and resale at another.

2 Commodities: Purchase of a contract in one delivery month and resale in another.

3 Euro-market, securities: difference between the rate at which a bank borrows money on inter-bank market and rate at which it on-lends funds to its customers.

STAG Someone who hopes to profit from a fixed-price issue of securities by asking for more than he wants. He hopes that the issue will be oversubscribed. He can then sell his surplus shares at a profit as soon as the secondary market trading begins.

STAND-BY ARRANGEMENT Members of the International Monetary Fund have the right to borrow from the fund a certain percentage of the quota that has been allocated to them. The arrangement indicates the amount they can borrow, when, for how long and under what terms. 25% of quotas can be borrowed with no strings attached.

STANDBY COMMITMENT A bank commitment to lend money up to a specific amount for a specific period, to be used only in a certain contingency.

STANDBY EQUITY In investment an agreement that is conditional on stock purchase.

STANDBY LETTER OF CREDIT A letter of credit issued to cover against a particular contingency.

STANDBY LOAN Loan which is not part of the current schedule but which can be presented to the board if another project slips.

'STAR TREK' ISSUE Eurodollar issue where interest rates have been set too low to attract investors. Called so because they are priced 'where no man dared to go'.

STATELESS MONEY Money which is not part of the currency of any country. Eurocurrency deposits as an example.

STATEMENT OF CHANGES IN FINANCIAL POSITION, CHANGES IN WORKING CAPITAL STATEMENT A statement used in conventional accounting which summarizes the financing and investing activities of an entity, including the extent to which the enterprise has generated funds from operations during the period and for completing the disclosure of changes in financial position during the period.

STEP-DOWN Securities where the coupon rate decreases by fixed amount every year.

STEPPED (RATE) BOND Bond with different coupon rates of interest for different periods, fixed in advance of the issue.

STEP-UP (SECURITY) Securities where the coupon rate increases by fixed amount every year.

STOCKBROKER A member of the stock exchange authorized to deal in securities.

STOCK DILUTION, STOCK WATERING The lessening of an ownership share's earnings and assets equity, caused by the issue of more ownership shares without corresponding increases in earnings and assets.

STOCK EXCHANGE The physical place where securities are bought and sold (in French: *bourse*).

STOCKHOLDERS' EQUITY, SHAREHOLDERS' EQUITY, OWNERS' EQUITY, EQUITY, NET WORTH, SHAREHOLDERS' FUNDS The value of assets less liabilities of a corporation. The terms given here are generally synonymous but accountants tend to give slants to these terms in certain circumstances, thus having at times different meanings.

STOCK INDEX FUTURE Security that combines features of traditional commodity futures trading with securities trading using composite stock indexes. Investors can speculate on general market performance or can buy an index future contract to hedge a long position or short position against a decline in value.

STOCK MARKET CRASH A major fall in stock prices (eg in 1929, 1987, 2000 and 2008).

STOCK OPTION A right granted by a corporation, usually to employees or underwriters, to purchase corporate stock, under specific price and timing conditions.

STOCK WARRANT Warrant to purchase stock.

STOP ORDER Order to buy or sell below a specified price, if reached.

STOP-OUT PRICE Uniform auction price at a Dutch auction (lowest price at which bids are accepted).

STRAIGHT BOND Bond with unquestioned right of principal at a specified future date, unquestioned right to fixed interest payments on stated dates and no right to any additional interest, principal or conversion privilege.

STRAIGHT, TAP CERTIFICATE OF DEPOSIT Standard certificate of deposit, without any restrictions on amount available.

STRANGLE An options strategy in which the exercise price of the call is higher, and that of the put lower, than the current price of the underlying stock.

STRIKING PRICE, STRIKE PRICE, EXERCISE PRICE Price a particular share must reach before an option to purchase shares can be exercised.

STRIP CERTIFICATE A security certificate that has had the coupon removed by a broker who sells it separately.

STRIP OF MATURITIES A time portion of each of the maturities of a multi-maturity loan.

STRIP PARTICIPATION Participation in each of the maturities of a multi-maturity loan.

STRIPPING Separation of future coupon payments and principal redemption values.

SUBBORROWER A smaller loan which is a part of a larger loan, often one provided for on-lending.

SUBLOAN A loan that has been on-lent.

SUBORDINATED LOAN A loan where repayment is made subject to other conditions being met, normally of other loans which are deemed to be 'senior' (often because they are secured).

SUBORDINATE LENDER Lender holding a subordinated loan.

SUPPLIER CREDIT A loan to a buyer or importer (for up to 80% of the purchase price of the goods purchased) which is guaranteed by the export credit agency of the country of the exporter.

SUSHI BOND Eurodollar bonds issued by Japanese corporations on the Japanese market for Japanese investors.

SUSPENSE ACCOUNT A sort of dustbin account (at a bank or elsewhere) into which payments are shunted temporarily while in transit or when there is doubt about the rightful home.

SWAP (TRANSACTION) A spot purchase of foreign exchange (currency swap), fixed or floating rate funds (interest rate swaps) or assets (asset swaps) with simultaneous forward sale or vice versa. In France: *credit croisé*, a transaction in which two partners swap financial assets.

SWINGLINE A short term line of credit enabling borrowers to draw at short notice to cover the delay in issuing notes or making other forms of drawing.

SWITCH Sale of paper which is no longer considered to have long-term possibilities and investment of the proceeds in securities considered more worthwhile.

SWITCHING VALUE The value that reverses the ranking of a project and its alternative.

SYNDICATE A group of bankers and/or brokers who underwrite and distribute a new issue of securities or a large block of an outstanding issue.

SYNDICATED LOAN Loan made by a syndicate of a large number of banks.

SYNTHETIC FLOATING NOTES, DERIVATIVE FLOATING RATE NOTES A name for asset swaps which are artificially packaged and marketed by investment banks rather than investors themselves.

T

TAKE-AND-PAY CONTRACT A guarantee to buy an agreed amount of a product or service provided it is delivered.

TAKE IN, TO (BILLS) Rediscount operation with the promise to transfer the credit title back to the original lender.

TAKE-OR-PAY CONTRACT An unconditional guarantee to buy an agreed amount of a product or service whether or not it is delivered.

TAKEOVER BID An offer to acquire a controlling interest in a corporation.

TAKEOVER CANDIDATE, TARGET COMPANY Company considered ripe for takeover.

TANKOKU BILL Six month bill issued by the Japanese government to refinance expiring long-term bonds.

TAP SECURITY, TAP STOCK Security that is continuously available and may be obtained on demand by investors (used primarily in the British market), released in parts, not all at once.

TARGETED CURRENCY POOL Now called 'Valuation Basket'. A 'basket' of currencies (including the US dollar, the Euro, Japanese Yen and Pound Sterling) are used to calculate an artificial currency unit called SDR, used by several international organisations. The valuation basket is reviewed and adjusted every five years.

TAX-ANTICIPATION NOTE, TAN Short-term borrowing issued to fill temporary financing needs. It is backed by anticipated tax receipts and any unencumbered revenue of the community.

TAX BUOYANCY Total elasticity of the tax system (built-in elasticity due to discretionary changes in the tax system). Measured by the annual mean growth in receipts divided by the annual mean growth in gross domestic product (GDP).

TAX CREDIT A 100% offset against tax liability.

TECHNICAL DECLINE, DROP The fall in price of a security or commodity because of factors relating to operation of the market and not because of any supply or demand condition.

TED SPREAD Technically, the spread between US Treasury bill futures and Eurodollar futures but commonly used to refer to the spot market yield spread between Treasury bills and LIBOR.

TELEGRAPHIC TRANSFER Telex or cable sent by a bank to its correspondent bank in another country requesting payment to a named beneficiary in that country.

TENDER OFFER A method of selling securities all over the world. The seller sets a price (tender price) at which he is prepared to sell securities. Offers are invited and applicants state what price they are prepared to pay. Nothing below the tender price is accepted. After a specified time the securities go to the highest bidder. If enough bids above the tender price have been received, the offer lapses and the whole issue can be withdrawn.

TENDER PANEL In a Euro-note issue, a group of banks separate from but usually with many members in the group of underwriters. The panel members bid for any notes issued, up to a predetermined maximum spread. The underwriters take up notes not bid for or extend loans of an equivalent amount. The tender panel banks expect to place paper they receive rather than hold it themselves.

TEN K A very detailed report and accounts which quoted companies have to file with the SEC (Securities and Exchange Commission) in the USA every year. It is more comprehensive than a company's annual report and accounts to shareholders; it is a fount of information for investigative journalists and takeover speculators.

TENOR The period of debt rescheduling in number of years.

TERM LOAN Medium- or long-term loan undertaken by a corporation when it cannot or does not want to issue a loan on the financial market. A five year loan will be granted for five years though repayments may be made throughout the period.

TERM SHEET List of terms and conditions for a loan.

TERM TRANSFORMATION The use of funds from short-term deposits to make long-term loans.

THIRD MARKET, OFF-THE-BOARD MARKET Market for security dealing in over-the-counter stocks listed on a stock exchange but between firms that are not members of an exchange and therefore do not charge regular listed commission.

THRIFTS General name for those financial institutions in the USA that have the word 'savings' as the first or second word in their title, eg 'Savings and loan associations' and 'mutual savings banks'.

TICK A movement in the price quotation of a security or contract.

TIGRS Names as a result of Euro-market's fondness for acronyms. TIGRS is short for Treasury Investment Gross Receipts. TIGRS are similar to CATS, Certificates of Accrual on Treasury Securities.

TIME ARBITRAGE Buying and selling at different maturities.

TIME DEPOSIT A bank deposit with a specified maturity eg three months, six months or a year.

TIMES INTEREST EARNED Net operating income divided by interest charges. Should be 1.0 or better.

TIME-SLICE LOAN Loan where a lender only finances the loan a part of the time.

TOMBSTONE Advertisement which announces that a credit has been arranged or a bond issue made. They are advertisements that adorn glossy financial magazines listing banks which have participated in a syndicated loan or bond issue. The pecking order on the tombstone is all important. At the top comes the name of the borrower and the amount and terms of the borrowing. Underneath come the banks. The size of the typeface in which their names appear corresponds to their importance in the deal. The more prestigious the borrower, the keener are the banks to show off on a tombstone. The less prestigious the borrower, the keener he is to show off the names of the banks that are prepared to lend to him. In the final analysis it is up to the borrower whether a tombstone advertisement appears. He pays for it.

TOPPING UP Providing extra funds to an existing loan package, rather than a new one.

TOP-RATED BOND Bond issued by corporation or organization considered to be particularly creditworthy.

TOWN CLEARING A system of clearing cheques between banks within the City of London more quickly than via the 'general clearing': the system for clearing non-city cheques.

TRADE BILL (UK) Commercial bill accepted directly by a corporation.

TRADE CREDIT Credit granted by one trader to another. If the trader is exporting, the trade credit becomes an export-credit.

TRADE DATE Date on which counter-parties commit to swap.

TRADE FINANCING FACILITY A financing arrangement by commercial creditors in the form of linking financing to particular projects or trade operations in countries where they have long-term business interests. These facilities enable banks to maintain closer ties with customers in both the debtor countries and industrial countries, while providing additional finance for a country's imports.

TRADE INSIDE FEE Said of a security traded at a price between the offering price and the offering price less the fees charged.

TRADER Individual who buys and sells stock for own profit or for a corporation.

TRANCHE The parts in which a loan is paid out if it is not all given to the borrower at once. Used mostly to refer to the parts in which the International Monetary Fund gives out its loans to member countries. Release of the next tranche of such a loan may be dependent on the borrowers' reaching prearranged economic targets.

TRANCHE CERTIFICATE OF DEPOSIT Certificate of deposit representing a share in a programme of certificate of deposit issues by a bank.

TRANCHING Division of a loan into several tranches. Release of tranches is conditional on specific agreed actions being carried out.

TRANSFERABLE SHARE Share of stock on which there are no restrictions on transfer of ownership.

TRANSFER PRICE Price between a corporation and its subsidiary or within a corporation (opposite of arm's length price).

TRANSFORMATION Medium- or long-term reinvestment operations by financial intermediaries, taking in liquid savings or sight deposits.

TRAVELLER'S CHEQUE A sort of cash substitute acceptable almost everywhere. Its secret is the simple security device of double signature. This gives the acceptor of the cheque a reasonably sophisticated guarantee that the person signing the cheque in front of him is the person who originally bought it.

TREASURY BILL (US) Bill issued by US Treasury with short maturity (less than one year) usually repayable in three months. In Britain they are issued every week (on Friday). The issue is always fully underwritten by the discount houses. Treasury bills are sold at a discount, their yield being a leading indicator of the way interest rates are moving.

TREASURY BOND (US) Long-term (more than ten years) fixed coupon paper issued by the Federal Reserve on behalf of the US Treasury.

TREASURY INVESTMENT GROWTH RECEIPT, TIGER Form of zero-coupon security first created by Merrill Lynch. They consist of US

Government-backed bonds that have been stripped of their coupons.

TREASURY NOTE A medium-term (two to ten years) coupon security issued by the US Treasury. In France *bons du trésor* have a maturity of one to five years.

TRIANGLE CONFIGURATION Form of bar chart used in analysis of securities where lines drawn round the chart have the shape of a triangle. There are three main varieties: symmetrical, ascending and descending. The symmetrical triangle is made up of two positive forces, buying and selling, while the ascending one indicates a positive buying force but a neutral selling force. Descending indicates a positive selling force but a neutral buying one.

TRIGGER Banks rarely give loans with no strings attached. The strings often take the form of conditions to be met by the borrower. If these conditions are not met then the bank's right to call in the loan (to get the money back) may be triggered.

TRIGGER CLAUSE Clause in IBRD loan agreement requiring review after a certain number of years to determine whether changes in the country's economic condition warrant harder or softer loans.

TRIGGER RATE Rate at which floating rate notes are automatically converted to fixed rate.

TROY OUNCE Measure used for weighing gold and silver, equal to 1.09714 non-Trojan ounces.

TRUE AND FAIR A much loved phrase of accountants. It is what they try to ensure in the accounts that they prepare or audit. This concept is more applicable to the boxing ring than to the accounts of companies. The true and fair view of a company's financial position is rarely, if ever, unique.

TRUNCATION System of limiting the physical circulation of securities in certificate form to save paper and reduce operating costs. Includes use of computers, microfiche etc.

TRUST BANK (SHINTAKU GINKO-JAPAN) Japanese bank involved in both lending and money management.

TRUSTEE A person who is entrusted with property belonging to someone else. He can act in different roles, as a person charged with disposing of a dead man's property according to his will (banks often do) or as the person charged with looking after the interests of a minor until he or she becomes of age, as a person charged with looking after money donated to a charity or looking after the editorial integrity and independence of a journal.

TURN The profit made from 'turning over' a particular bit of business. For a bank it is the amount it earns from charging a higher rate of interest to the borrower than it pays to depositors. The difference between the rates of interest for borrowers and depositors is known as 'spread'.

TWO-POINT ARBITRAGE, SPACE ARBITRAGE Buying in one centre and selling in another.

TWO-TIER MARKET An exchange rate regime which normally insulates a country from the balance of payments effects of capital flows while it maintains a stable exchange rate for current account transactions. Capital transactions are normally required to pass through a 'financial' market while current transactions go through an 'official' market, though other arrangements are possible. Examples are found in Belgium and the UK but France and Italy also have experimented with the system.

U

●●●●●●●●●●●●●●●●●●●●●●●●●●●●●●●●●●

UNBUNDLING OF FINANCIAL RISKS The separation of evaluation of financial risks.

UNCALLED CAPITAL The amount of capital by which the total capital authorized by the stockholders exceeds the paid-up capital.

UNDERLYING (SECURITY) Security or other instrument that must be delivered if an option is exercised.

UNDERWRITE To agree to buy the whole of a bond or a share issue.

UNDERWRITER The middleman for selling and distributing securities to investors or the public. If he cannot sell the securities (ie when the price is not right) he will be left holding them for longer than he hoped.

UNIT-MANAGED COSTS Costs which are the responsibility, for budget purposes, of individual units, as opposed to those that are centrally managed.

UNIT TRUST A British form of investment designed to widen share ownership. Unit trusts invest money in shares and other marketable debt on behalf of small investors. An investor holds a unit in the trust, the value of that unit reflecting the value of the shares lying behind it. Units trusts differ from investment trusts in that every time more money is put into the unit trust, more 'units' are issued. The only way an investor can buy into an investment trust is to buy its existing shares. The theoretical advantage of a unit trust is that it enables small investors to have a wider portfolio than if they were investing on their own and at a lower cost.

UNIVERSAL BANK(ING) Bank providing the full range of banking services.

UNLISTED (SECURITY) Security not listed for trading on one of the regular stock exchanges and which is, therefore, traded directly or over the counter.

UNREALIZED GAINS Profits that have not become actual. The gains are realized when the security or other instrument on which there has been a gain is sold for a profit.

UNSEASONED INVESTMENT Investment that is not yet fully producing.

UNSECURED CREDIT A loan that has no security. If a borrower goes bust, the provider of unsecured credit has to wait until all the secured creditors have taken their bite before he has any right to whatever assets are left.

UNWIND Reverse a securities transaction through an offsetting transaction.

USUANCE DRAFT A draft payable on some specific future date. To be distinguished from a sight draft.

UTILIZATION FEE Fee paid for use of a Euro-note facility.

VALUE DATE Calendar date on which a transaction takes place.

VALUE IMPAIRED Refers to a loan which is doubtful. US banking authorities are obliged by law to declare loans with overdue interest in excess of six months as *value impaired.*

VANILLA SWAP *See Plain vanilla swap.*

VARIABLE COST Costs that vary directly with the level of activity. Examples include costs of moving cargo inland on trains or trucks, stevedoring in some ports, short term equipment leases.

VARIABLE RATE Interest rate that varies in line with a benchmark, like LIBOR. It is the American expression for 'floating rate' and the opposite of 'fixed rate'.

VENTURE CAPITAL Financing which involves a relatively high risk. Many believe this will prime the pump for the next industrial revolution. It is capital put up by individuals or financial institutions to back risky industrial and commercial ventures at the beginnings of their lives. Many already have suffered heavily after the last 'high tech' bust.

VENTURE CAPITAL COMPANY Company specializing in providing venture capital.

VERGLEICH Germany's form of receivership ie half way to bankruptcy. Strict conditions are required. When accepted, the company can write off up to 65% of all its debts before carrying on almost as before. First a company must be unable to pay its bills. Then, if half of the company's creditors, representing 80% of its debts, agree, a court can approve *Vergleich.* The company's debts are frozen for 18 months if it agrees to pay back 35% of its debts, 24 months if it agrees to pay back 40%. In practice less than 1% of troubled companies make it.

VOLATILE STOCK Stock that changes in a manner inconsistent with changes in the rest of the market.

VOLATILITY RATIO Ratio by which overall changes in the stock market influence changes in a specific stock.

VOLUNTARY, SPONTANEOUS LENDING Lending that is made willingly, as opposed to lending where the lender has some sort of obligation to lend or else the borrower will not reimburse previous loans.

VOSTRO ACCOUNT Expression used between banks when referring to one another's account. From Latin *voster* = your. Your account with us.

W

WAIVER The agreement of a lender to overlook a borrower's failure to meet certain conditions attached to receiving a loan and without which the loan would be 'in default'. Waivers are given for a short period, aiting for the borrower to meet the conditions.

WAIVER OF NEGATIVE PLEDGE, NEGATIVE PLEDGE WAIVER Situation whereby a lender waives his right to a negative pledge in a loan agreement (ie an agreement that the borrower will not pledge any of his assets if doing so would result in less security to the lender covered under the agreement).

WAREHOUSING Disguising purchase of shares in a company by using nominees and others to buy stakes. In this way a surprise takeover bid can be done. Some countries try to stop this by requiring public disclosure of any stake over 5% held in a company and by issuing rules about the attitude of concert parties.

WARRANT Option to purchase ordinary share or bond of a particular company, usually purchased by bond-holder wanting to participate in profit growth of that company. Often attached to new bond issue as inducement for investors to take up the bond.

WARRANT BOND Bond with warrant attached. This may be a bond with bond-warrant or with equity-warrant.

WARRANT INTO GOVERNMENT SECURITIES, WINGS Warrant which allows the purchaser to acquire, within a specified period of time, at a fixed price, a US Treasury bill of specified coupon rate and maturity.

WASH SALE Occurs when a person buys and sells a stock, thereby recording a price, but with no actual change of ownership having taken place.

WATCH LIST List of securities singled out for special surveillance by a brokerage firm or exchange or other self-regulatory organization to spot irregularities. Firms on the list may be takeover candidates, companies about to issue new securities or those that seem to have attracted an unusually heavy volume of trading activity.

WHEN ISSUED (WI) SECURITY Security sold conditionally as, though it has been authorized, it has not yet been issued.

WHITE KNIGHT Someone appearing to rescue a company that is subject of a hostile takeover bid. He puts in a better offer and waits until the predator disappears. Sometimes also considered as a company which takes over another of which it does not know the real problems but considers it an 'opportunity' and burning its fingers as a result.

WHOLE LOAN SALE Sale of portions of individual loans in transactions negotiated directly with the end investors (typically banks).

WHOLESALE BANKING *1* Large-scale dealings in money deposits centred in the closely interrelated group of money markets which have developed since the mid-1960s.
2 Banking facilities offering a limited number of services to select clients (generally large corporations).

WINDOW Short-lived opportunity to issue securities that may be taken up by any of a significant number of highly rated borrowers.

WINDOW DRESSING Financial actions such as stock market trading, where the purpose is to make a corporation's financial situation seem better than it really is, just before the publication of a balance sheet or other financial statement.

WINGS Euro-speak for 'warrants' into negotiable government securities, a Euro-market instrument with a warrant attached, to buy American government securities.

WITHHOLDING TAX Any tax withheld at the source. Frequently imposed on bond interests and dividends and sometimes on bank interests. Tax collectors love this type of taxing because it makes their job easier and cuts down on tax evasion.

WOLFHOUND BOND Was a bond issued in Irish pounds on the Irish market by non-Irish borrowers.

WORKING CAPITAL The excess of current assets over current liabilities. The capital left to work in running day to day business. More than once companies have gone bankrupt because they have had insufficient working capital.

WORKING RATIO Total working expenses (all

operating expenses, before depreciation) divided by total operating revenues. The ratio should be well under 1.0.

WORKOUT ARRANGEMENTS, WORKOUTS Arrangements between borrowers and debtors (usually at international level) to extend repayment schedules and provide new credit at reduced interest rates.

WRIT A written order from a court commanding someone to do (or not to do) something.

WRITE-DOWN A partial write-off when a bank thinks that it may not be repaid in full.

WRITE OFF, CHARGE-OFF When an asset or a portion of an asset is recognized as worthless, it is removed from the books of a corporation and a corresponding loss in the corporation's capital is recognized.

YANKEE BOND Bond issued on the US market in US dollars outside the US.

YIELD Return on an investment expressed in percentage.

YIELD CURVE Graph relating rates of return to maturity.

YIELD CURVE ARBITRAGE Taking a position based on a view of expected changes in the shape of the yield curve independent from the general interest rate view as it is expressed by the average duration at which the portfolio is positioned.

YIELD PICKUP A currency hedged strategy where, because of the difference in shape of the yield curves of two currencies, the difference in interest rates between these two currencies is not reflected in forward exchange rates, giving arbitrage opportunities under which bonds of equivalent duration in these currencies can be swapped and the current exposure hedged.

YIELD TO MATURITY, YTM The return a security earns, assuming that it is held until a certain date and put to the borrower at the specified put price.

Z

ZERO COUPON BOND Bond that pays no interest but is sold at a steep discount and paid off at par.
ZERO COUPON EUROSTERLING BEARER REGISTERED ACCRUING SECURITY (ZEBRAs) Eurobond, denominated in sterling and sold at a steep discount.

ABOUT THE AUTHOR

After a seafaring career of seven years, Honoré C Paelinck moved to Antwerp to work in the ship repair and cargo handling business. He acted as a Technical Consultant to various ports in East Africa, and planned and oversaw the creation of a combined container and steel terminal in Antwerp.

In 1971 he moved to Africa to become General Manager of the ports of the Democratic Republic of the Congo, and after six years became Chairman and Managing Director of the National Transport Organization, which consisted of 3 sea ports, 71 inland ports, 4,400km of railways, 3 shipyards, 19 schools and more than 27,000 staff.

He returned to Belgium in 1985, and ran the Belgian National Railways for a short period before moving into private enterprise as a staff member of Van Ommeren, in charge of European inland shipping, stevedoring (international) and the Belgian holding.

In 1991 he became Managing Director of his own consulting firm, Port and Transport Consulting, and has since worked regularly for the World Bank, the European Commission and several international banking organizations and private enterprises.

He is also Guest Professor at UA, ITMMA and lecturer at a number of foreign universities; a member of the Royal Marine Academy and Chairman of the section Economics and Law; a member of the Royal Academy of Science in Belgium and member of the board of several private companies. He regularly writes articles on ports, economics and shipping.

OTHER TITLES IN THE REEDS PROFESSIONAL SERIES

REEDS SEA TRANSPORT
5th edition
Patrick M Alderton
978 0 7136 6944 2
Gives a complete picture of the maritime transport industry, taking into account recent changes, new data and statistics, new safety advice, a review of ship types and a new chapter on marine finance. Ideal for professionals as well as students.

REEDS MARINE INSURANCE
Barrie Jervis
978 0 7136 7396 8
Aimed at all those with little or no experience of marine or any other form of insurance working within the maritime transport field. Ideal for professionals as well as students of maritime law, sea transport and shipping.

REEDS MARINE SURVEYING
2nd edition
Thomas Ask
978 0 7136 7714 0
Covering the latest surveying technology, this expanded and updated edition also includes an analysis of the mechanical behaviour of materials and a useful checklist with practical techniques and hints for conducting a survey.

REEDS MARINE DISTANCE TABLES
11ᵗʰ edition
R W Caney and J E Reynolds
978 1 4081 2277 8
The perfect ready-reckoner for any navigator wanting a quick and accurate distance reference between all the regularly used ports around the world. Divided into key 'market areas', it includes a pull-out map for area identification, useful tables of major 'turning points', time zones and time and speed conversion tables.

REEDS MARITIME METEOROLOGY
Revised edition
Maurice Cornish and Elaine Ives
978 1 4081 1206 9
Gives descriptions of the elements and forces which contribute to maritime meteorology and the principles which govern them, accompanied by numerous explanatory photos and diagrams.